Delia...

...the influencers in her life and the lessons learned.

Martha D. Staker

Dear Diana + Bob
Wishing you a
Blessed & Happy New
Year - 2025!
Love,
Martha

Copyright © 2024 by Martha D. Staker
Paperback ISBN 9798346688549

All rights reserved. No part of this book may be reproduced, scanned, or distributed in any form, printed or electronic, without permission. Please do not participate in or encourage piracy of copyrighted materials, in violation of the author's rights.

Editing and technical assistance contributed by Gabrielle Rose Staker.

Cover picture from Marie Murphy, Rostrevor, County Down, Northern Ireland.

Contents

Acknowledgments	vii
Prologue	1
Introduction	5
My Story Begins	9
CHAPTER 1 *My Early Years: 1945 to 1950* Martha: Birth to Five Years of Age	11
CHAPTER 2 *1950 to 1955* Martha: 5-10 Years of Age	19
CHAPTER 3 *1955 to 1960* Martha: 10 to 15 Years of Age	37
My Grandparents as Influencers	51
CHAPTER 4 *1960 to 1965* Martha: 15-20 Years of Age	69
CHAPTER 5 *1965 to 1970* Martha: 20-25 Years of Age	85
CHAPTER 6 *1970 to 1975* Martha: 25 to 30 Years of Age	101
CHAPTER 7 *1975 to 1980* Martha: 30-35 Years of Age	113
CHAPTER 8 *1980 – 1985* Martha: 35 to 40 Years of Age	125
CHAPTER 9 *1985 to 1990* Martha: 40 to 45 Years of Age	151
CHAPTER 10 *1990 to 1995* Martha: 45 to 50 Years of Age	165

CHAPTER 11   177
1995-2000
Martha: 50 to 55 Years of Age

CHAPTER 12   185
2000 to 2005
Martha: 55 to 60 Years of Age

CHAPTER 13   201
2005-2010
Martha: 60 to 65 Years of Age

CHAPTER 14   209
2010 to 2015
Martha: 65 to 70 Years of Age

CHAPTER 15   217
The "Still" Years 2015 – 2020
Martha: 70 to 75 Years of Age

CHAPTER 16   229
The Unknown-Ten Years into the Future: 2020 to 2025
Martha: 75 to 85 Years of Age

Take Aways   231
Lessons from Seven Decades of Living   237

Historical Facts and Influencers   245

About the Author   265

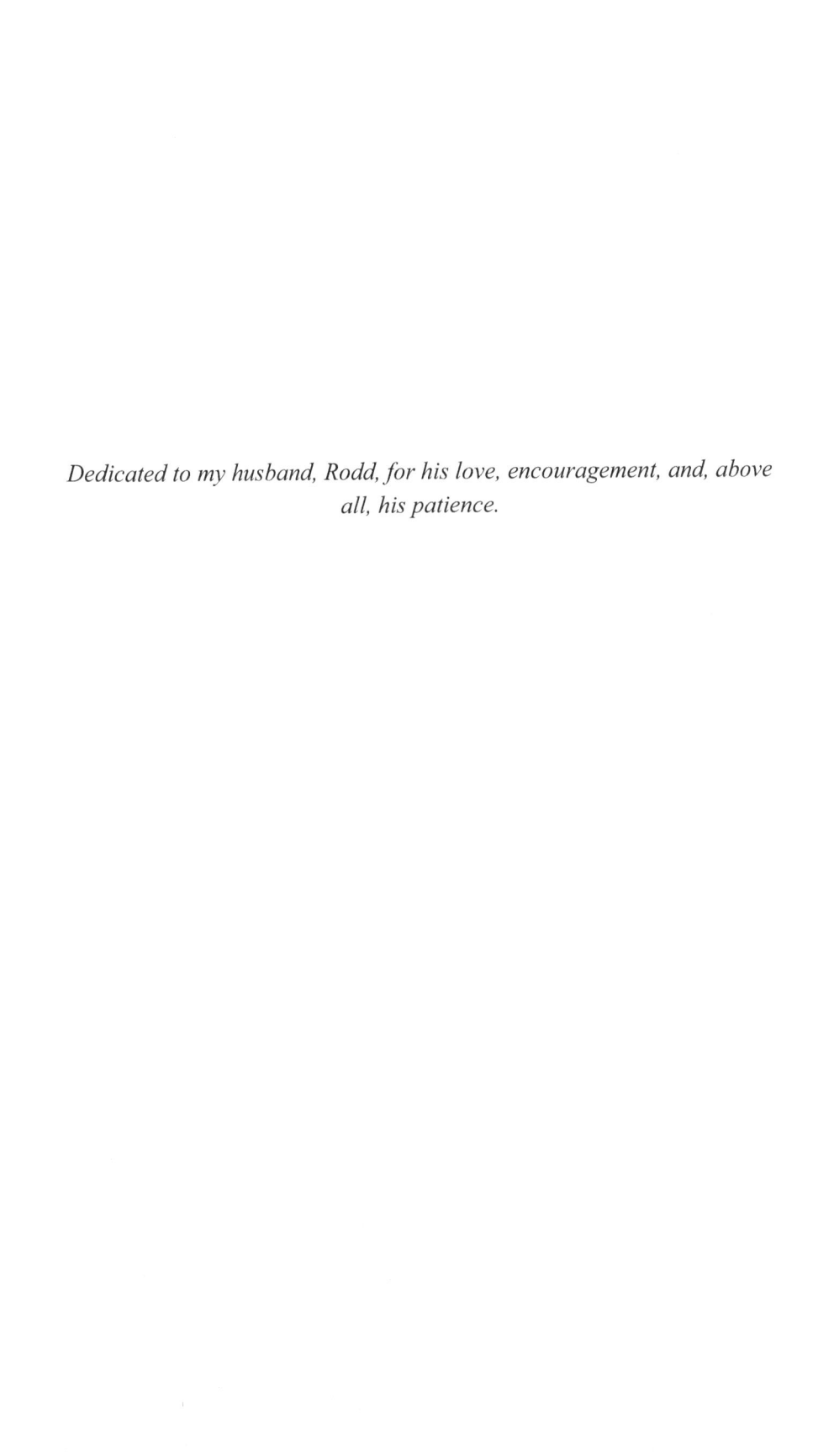

Dedicated to my husband, Rodd, for his love, encouragement, and, above all, his patience.

Acknowledgments

I am grateful to all those who pushed me, encouraged me, and influenced me to write:

My husband - my best friend. Rodd David encouraged me to do what I wanted. He never limited my efforts but rather championed my ideas. He never pushed me, rather listened, sometimes for hours, as I described my challenges and inner conflicts. He would say when I became frustrated (I am Irish), "Life is a marathon, not a sprint. Slow down and enjoy the ride." We took turns – he went to graduate school; I went to graduate school. He traveled around the world, and I traveled across the United States. Both of us growing – never competing – always wanting the best for each other.

My Children: I still hear my son's frequent harassment, "how's that book coming? Would you like Gabby (my 14-year-old granddaughter at the time) to help you? Most of all I am grateful for the memories and experiences my daughter and two sons provided me with. Many of the stories in this book are their stories, too.

My Siblings: My older brother, Bill, being three years older than myself, was able to verify or correct inaccuracies in the stories I remember about my ancestors. His help has been a treasure. I hope he enjoyed the process as much as I did. We have never been close throughout our lives, but now in our later years, we have found a way to work together and perhaps better understand each other. I am a better person for having had my siblings, Mary Helen, Bill, Michael, and Elizabeth Ann in my life. Our love and friendship grew as we got older.

Eunice Kennedy Shriver: What a woman, what a friend, what a mentor. She saw in me my willingness to question, to challenge ideas and traditional methodologies. She liked my persistence, my spunk and passion, and the fact that I would fight for what I believed. She mentored me for almost a decade. Whether traveling to Washington, DC to meet with Senators or speaking to the school district in New Haven, Connecticut, or Sacramento, California, or meeting with researchers like Dr. Robert Coles or Dr. Bill May, Mrs. Shriver exposed me to life experiences and people I had only read about. I am grateful for the memories. She was a very intense human being who never noticed that her skirt turned 360 degrees as she hurriedly marched across a university campus or around a city block sharing her thoughts with me. Mostly, she talked, and I listened.

My Niece: Mary Higgins Colucci. Mary is a remarkable woman. If it had not been for Mary researching our ancestry, I would never have met our dear extended family in Ireland. She has given me and our whole family a precious gift.

My friends: I have the greatest group of friends, some of which I have known since kindergarten. They have offered me solace, an escape from work and professional stressors, and a place to laugh without questions being asked. Together we celebrate the moment and traverse the highs and lows of each other's lives.

My Colleagues: I have been blessed to have worked with some of the smartest, wittiest, colleagues who stood by me in good and bad times and respected me when we disagreed on research methodologies and practices. How do women survive in today's world without an Allison Lundquist, Heather Schrotberger, Earl Thomas, Mary Davidson, Barb Friedmann and Bob Graham, Linda Hawley, or Shirley Goode in their lives? I learned so much by listening to those with whom I worked, and I will be forever grateful to the women and men who supported me.

PROLOGUE

I HAVE ALWAYS HAD an inner sense or belief that I was meant to do something out of the ordinary - something of significance in my lifetime. Living with this persistent conscious conviction has been unsettling and painful at times. I've asked others if they share this feeling and they have said no. Sensing my existential anxiety, my children have suggested that maybe I have already accomplished what I was meant to do. They are quick to remind me that I had birthed them. Obviously, my children have a high regard for themselves. I have been a good mother. I have had a successful career and been acknowledged for my accomplishments. Yet, I have never felt that I was done. I find myself questioning what is next, what is it that I still need to do, or maybe, what is it that I still want to do. When I recently talked with a counselor and told her I was thinking about going back to work, she said, "You have already done that." Five powerful words!

For years I publicly announced my intention to write a book. I was in fifth grade when I first recorded my desire to write. Mrs. Martin, the only lay teacher (non-nun) at Visitation Catholic grade school at the time, gave the class a writing assignment, i.e., write a one-page essay on what you want to be when you grow up. When it came my turn to read my paper in front of my classmates, I told Mrs. Martin I did not want to read my essay out loud. Mrs. Martin hesitantly said, "ok" but advised that no one else in the class was to ask to be excused from reading their report. Telling my classmates that I wanted to be a newspaper reporter was not what made me uncomfortable. It was the fact that I had written an essay saying that I wanted to be a fashion model and a newspaper reporter.

It might never have gotten to this point if I had not vocalized my career goals at my 20th high school reunion. Our class representative asked everyone to share what they had been doing the last 20 years and what their goals were going forward. There were only 52 girls in my high school graduating class and only half of them attended homecoming weekend. We were known at St. Teresa's Academy as the "Small but Mighty Class of

'62." When it came to my turn, I mentioned that my husband and I had three children, and I was currently teaching in the Department of Nursing at Avila College. Then I casually said without hesitation (and much fore thought) that my goals for the future included being on the Today Show and writing a best seller. Five years later, on the exact day I celebrated my 25th high school reunion I was on the Today Show, interviewed by Deborah Norville. So– where is the book?

What I didn't know at the time was that life was preparing me to write. A colleague, Helen Raikes, once asked me, "How important is it to you to write this book you keep talking about?" "It is very important," I replied. Not a day passes without me metaphorically recording the memories and life experiences that I recall most often, the influencers in my life and the life lessons those influencers taught me. Synchronicity is everywhere. Everything I read, listen to or see on TV reminds me, nags me, urges me, inspires me to sit at the computer and write.

I have postponed my urge to write rationalizing I had time, but my time is running out. If I am going to tell my story, I need to overcome my fear of sharing what's inside of me - and discipline myself to do it.

I think my reluctance can be likened to a story from Alfred Benjamin's book, "The Helping Interview." One evening on his way home from work a stranger walking down the street asked Alfred for directions. Alfred was careful in explaining the directions and even asked the stranger if he understood. The stranger assured him that he had and turned and walked away. Mr. Benjamin called after him and told him he was going in the wrong direction. The stranger said, "I know, I'm not quite ready yet."[1]

Now it's TIME and I'm Finally Ready. I am determined to do what I said I would do. I do not want to go 6 feet under or be scattered in the garden while people whisper, "Martha never did write that book she was always talking about. It was just a lot of bull____."

I believe that writing is the uncomfortable, unknown, undone part of my life that has been obstructing my gracious acknowledgement of aging. The poet, Maya Angela in her book, *I Know Why the Caged Bird Sings*, said,

"There is no greater agony than bearing an untold story inside you." So it is with this truth I now share my story for the first time hoping it will enrich the lives of those I love and others.

Photos of Martha acting like a Model

Age 3

Age 4

Age 6

Age 9

---

1. Benjamin, A. (1981). *The Helping Interview* (Third). Houghton Mifflin Company.

INTRODUCTION

In 1983, I was coordinating prenatal care and social services (including nutritional and exercise classes) for pregnant and parenting teens as part of a federal grant awarded to St. Mary's Hospital in Kansas City, Missouri. Eunice Kennedy Shriver, the Executive Director of the Joseph P. Kennedy, Jr. Foundation, in Washington, D.C., learned of my work and efforts from a federal project officer and invited me to submit a grant proposal to the Foundation. Mrs. Shriver was President John F. Kennedy's sister. President Kennedy was someone I supported and believed in back in the early 60's. Now there was the possibility that I could work with President Kennedy's sister and receive funding from the Joseph P. Kennedy, Jr. Foundation. The small grant of $9,000 would enhance my knowledge and skills for working with teens. Mrs. Shriver and her team of experts had created a curriculum for pregnant and parenting teens called "Community of Caring" and believed if young pregnant teens received comprehensive prenatal care and education within a caring community, the teen mothers and their babies would have improved outcomes and there would be fewer babies born with special needs.

I was awarded the $9,000 grant and within two weeks I was on my way to Washington, DC to study and learn from the scholars and researchers Eunice Kennedy Shriver convened. Mrs. Shriver believed those working with teens needed to know what they themselves valued before they could help teens work through a values-based curriculum. The first day of the forum I was introduced to a simple paper and pen exercise – **the Life Time Line.** This exercise asked me to write down the three most critical life experiences/memories that I recall for every 5-year period of my life. Then I was prompted to identify the value or lesson learned from each experience/memory. From this exercise, I gained a deeper understanding of how one's life experiences shape one's future behavior and collectively shape one's character and philosophy of life. The **Life Time Line** exercise helped me identify those people in my life and those life experiences that helped me- intentionally or not - become the person I am today. These were the people and/or experiences that taught me some of the most important life lessons and to whom I am most grateful.

As a result of this simple paper and pen exercise, the process of "reflecting" became an intentional part of my daily life. It has always been easy for me to recall life events. Most of my life, I have been driven and motivated more by external factors than internal ones, which caused me to be more alert and aware of what was happening around me. What others thought of me and the context within which I worked were both motivating and anxiety inducing.

Over the next 8 years as a consultant for the Joseph P. Kennedy, Jr. Foundation, I traveled across the country helping others learn how to reflect on their most significant memories and thus identify what it is they value.

Before one can be successful in life, think critically, or imagine changing the world for the better, one needs to know who one is and what it is they value. Once you know this, you have a foundation – a footing – and can move forward with confidence. Others will listen to you because you are authentic and real. People will see that in you. It is more than value signaling, it is value living.

The purpose of this book is multifold.

- To reflect on the influencers in my life, from birth to old age, and how they shaped the person I became and the values I freely choose to act on. Influencers include people, places, events, and things.
- To demonstrate that the greatest influencers in our lives are not necessarily the big events like marriage, Christmas, birthdays, the prom, or even the birth of a child. Rather, they're the small things, often the incidental word, conversation, or experience which plant a seed or question within us and work their way into our consciousness helping to define who we become.
- To offer a rubric for others who want to better understand themselves and the direction of their own life.

It is not hubris that drives me to write this book, but a humble belief that my story will make a difference. The book is formatted to encourage the reader to record his or her life experiences alongside my most important memories/experiences, that I identify within a historical context. In such a complicated world where truth seems eclipsed, this book may offer personal clarity and peace.

People say they are looking for balance in their lives, but how can anyone achieve balance in his or her life if they can't articulate what it is they value and how they want to spend their time? Knowing what we value and how it affects our decisions and actions is a necessary step in giving meaning to our lives. In a recent article, "Busyness Is Laziness," Joshua Becker wrote, "A busy life is an unexamined life. And an unexamined life is rarely worth living."[1]

In our rush to "live our best life," some of us have forgotten basic tenets. One of those tenets is acting on a set of values and beliefs and having those values reinforced by the major influencers in our lives. Growing up I learned values from my parents, grandparents, through my catholic education, teachers and friends. I watched TV shows like *Sky King* and *Little House on the Prairie, the Brady Bunch, Mr. Rodgers* and *Howdie Doody*. Recently I found myself becoming friends with Ryder, Mayor Goodway, and all the friendly and helpful dogs in *Paw Patrol*. I found myself watching a sitcom, *The Neighborhood*, where a white couple moves into a black neighborhood. Life lessons and values are at the heart of each show. These TV shows emphasize good over evil, doing the right thing, helping others in trouble, having fun, and loving those around you. Today, many TV shows reflect the darker side of what is happening in our world and unfortunately money and ratings drive most media decisions. Sharing one's values these days may get TV producers and sponsors sued or worse. They could lose their jobs.

Reflection can be emotionally painful. Writing and recalling certain memories was hard for me at times. I still feel pain when I recall that no one in our family attended my younger brother's high school graduation or the years no one in my family spoke to me. However, the light comes from knowing that those experiences changed me for the better- made me the mother, grandmother, wife, woman I am today.

Here I am, in my seventh decade of life, sharing my stories and what I believe is important to pass down. I hope I will inspire you to do the same. Sharing this exercise and my story is the most important treasure I can leave to my children, my friends, and those in search of their truth.

At this point, I was going to begin by telling you that my life was not an extraordinary one, rather a modest life where I believed if I worked hard and prayed, things would work out. But as I think about it, my life was and is extraordinary. So is your life! We have each been given a life with extraordinary purpose.

---

1. Becker, J. (n.d.). Busyness is laziness. *The Epoch Times*, pp. 4–5.

MY STORY BEGINS

(Imparting the Most Significant Memories and Influencers in My Life Within a Historical Context)

I was born on January 30, 1945. It was such a cold and snowy January that Dr. Singleton decided to send me and my mother home from the hospital in an ambulance when I was 10 days old. My mother had taken good care of me during the nine months I developed in her womb and my birth went smoothly. I was a healthy nine-pound baby girl that had excellent Apgar scores and, according to the obstetrical nurses, had strong vocal cords that broadcast loudly to the world that I arrived

There were a lot of people waiting to meet me, people that brought their life experiences and values to bear on me, all of which I would store within me and recall throughout my life. For good or bad, with truth or misunderstanding, with naivety and innocence, I grew up.

Chapter 1

My Early Years: 1945 to 1950
Martha: Birth to Five Years of Age

My full legal name is Martha Delia Leahy Staker. I was the third of five children born to William James Leahy, Jr., and Mary Elizabeth Callahan who married on September 10th, 1938, at Our Lady of Good Counsel Church. My older siblings, Mary Helen, age 5, and Billy (William James, III) age 2 ½, were staying with my maternal grandmother, while I was born. Grandma was anxious to meet me, so a few days after I was home, she placed my sister and brother in her Model T Ford and headed south on Summit, down the steep hill overlooking the Country Club Plaza (811 West 45th St.) and across 47th Street to Troost Avenue. Their destination was 5330 Troost. My brother, Billy, still recalls the perilous trip over snowbanks and slick streets as grandma, an infrequent driver, traversed the landscape. At 2 ½ Billy never forgot that day. I was named for Grandma Delia, a no-nonsense hardworking woman from the north of Ireland who I never remember seeing smile or laugh during the 14 years I knew her. Didi, as I affectionately called her, would inspire me.

I came home to a small two-bedroom home with an upstairs sleeping porch that I shared with my two older siblings. Rockhurst High School was across the street. It was a family neighborhood with the streetcar running down the middle of Troost Avenue and students racing to get to school or classes on time. My older siblings walked to their piano lessons and the milk truck came by each day. Neighbors borrowed a cup of sugar or a stick of butter. Flowers bloomed in most yards, and we were close enough to Grandma Didi's that we could visit often. Most fathers were missing from the neighborhood at the time since they had been drafted to fight in World War II. This created some animosity in the neighborhood since my dad didn't have to go to war. Working within the grain industry, his job was deemed critical to the supply chain that fed the soldiers fighting across the sea. We were blessed to have dad at home with us.

I have a few memories from my early years. Sometimes it is hard to distinguish between what I remember and what others told me. Or maybe it was seeing a picture of myself at a young age that created a memory. However, I do remember the mumps, the chicken pox, and having my tonsils removed at Menorah Hospital. I stayed in a crib with side rails and had lots of popsicles. I remember getting cut by a sickle as my older brother was "mowing" the tall grass in the front yard of our home and then getting an ice cream cone at Adam's corner drug store that evening to help the hurt go away.

I remember the car door being shut on my fingers and crying. My fingers were purple and red. I also remember sticking my first two fingers into the ends of the old rusty red scooter's handlebars near a lamppost on Troost Avenue and not being able to get them out. I remember Grandma sitting with my mother at the dining room table, darning socks, and mending clothes.

I remember my little brother being born sooner than expected and Dad holding Michael who had bandages on his eyes for days after eye surgery. I remember moving to a bigger home in the Brookside area when I was barely five and riding my tricycle on the front porch. I remember a neighbor boy chasing me, and I fell forward over a driveway curb and had a concussion.

I remember my dad sitting in the living room in a big chair by the west window at night and telling me and my siblings stories. We always begged for the same stories, Little Red Riding Hood and The Three Little Pigs. Dad loved to tickle us as he played like the wolf and then he would get down on all fours and let us ride on his back as he tried to bump us off. It was a fun time. I loved those times and stories.

My parents, William James Leahy, Jr., and Mary Elizabeth Callahan were married on September 10, 1938. Joe Leahy, my dad's younger brother, is on the far right next to Rose Bauman, my mother's first cousin, and Maid of Honor.

Pictures of Siblings taken between the years of 1946 and 1952.

Clockwise from the Top (L to R): Martha, Billy, Mary Helen, Elizabeth Ann, and Michael Daniel. Formal portraits and family pictures became less frequent after my aunt Tootsie died. She had the camera and the money to make sure pictures would reflect our early years.

Major influencers and the lessons I was learning at this stage of my life:

Although I was a busy preschooler, a little sister and big sister, I frequently recall three times in my early years that I believe influenced who I was to become and what I value.

- I was standing next to the bassinet and staring at my little brother. I was 3 years old, and Michael Daniel was a newborn, born prematurely at 7 months gestation. My mother looked down at me and said, "Martha, I need to run up the street to Carrol Grocery and get spaghetti noodles for dinner. I want you to stand there next to the bassinet and watch Michael. Don't move. Just stand there and I will be back in 5 minutes." Carrol Grocery was at 55th and Troost, one and a half blocks from our home. I remember standing there for what seemed like a long time. Then mother came in the door, smiled, and told me I did a good job. I had not moved but just stared at Michael the whole time while he slept.

I learned: to **take directions** and do what I was asked to do. Mother could **trust** me. I was trustworthy. Mother provided opportunities for me to learn **responsibility** at an early age.

- I was 3 years old. It was Sunday morning, and our family was walking home from St. Francis Xavier Catholic Church after mass. It was less than a block away from our home. It was sunny, but cold. I had on my winter coat and bonnet that tied under my chin. My dad reached down and took my hand in his. His hand was warm and he wrapped it around mine. We walked home together. I can still feel the warmth of his hand when I close my eyes.

Dad **loved** me and **cared** for me. I felt **safe**. I was happy. I was learning that **Family** is important.

- One day I decided to run away from home. I went down the street and around the corner walking west to Harrison Street. As I stood there a woman pushing a stroller passed and spoke to me. She said she was going to the grocer. I have no idea how long I stayed there but long enough for the woman to return from the grocer and give me a box of animal crackers. Then I went home and told everyone what I had done. No one had missed me. I didn't get into trouble.

Perhaps this was the start of **self-determination** and the beginning of **independence.**

I was also learning at this time:

Getting ice cream or a **treat can make a hurt better.**

Avoid bullies, you can get hurt.

The reader's personal reflections and influencers from birth to five years of age:

Chapter 2

1950 to 1955

Martha: 5-10 Years of Age

I GREW UP in a family that valued education – despite our family history of alcoholism, hoarding of outgrown clothes and hand-me-downs reminiscent of the Great Depression, and regular discussion of global threats around the kitchen table. My parents decided to spend their money to send me and my siblings to the "best" Catholic schools in Kansas City. They believed that education was everything. I grew up understanding that college was the place you went to right after high school, and there were no other options.

Even as both my parents set high aspirations for their children, their reasons for valuing education differed. Mother lamented her lack of education her whole life and projected her educational aspirations onto the next generation of women, me and my two sisters. My mother had attended Good Council Catholic grade school and then enrolled in the three-year high school business track offered at Redemptorist High School. More than anything, my mother wanted a four-year high school diploma, to take physical education with the other girls, and become a nurse at the University of Kansas Medical Center. As a teenager, mother had to be hospitalized at the University of Kansas Medical Center, diagnosed with a "goiter," and needed a thyroidectomy. She thought it would be exciting to be a nurse.

My grandma Didi had a different plan for my mother. She wanted her daughter to have skills, like typing and shorthand, so she could get a job, go to work, and earn money. She prioritized a catholic education, but she wouldn't spend the money for my mother to get a four- year high school education, or "put out" the extra 75 cents a semester that it cost to take physical education. My mother lived with the constant reminder of the poverty her parents experienced growing up in Ireland, and her parents vowed to never be poor again. Grandma viewed a vocational education as a step up since she herself cleaned other peoples' homes, cared for their children, and waited tables.

My dad on the other hand loved school and received a satisfying education at Rockhurst High School which was located at 52nd and Troost Avenue at the time. Dad was enrolled in the Honor's tract of studies. It didn't matter if it was Greek, Latin, English, or Mathematics, all his classes came easy. Dad was "brilliant". Since he didn't have to study a whole lot, he had time to pursue his other ambition: having fun. It is my understanding that my dad would have been class Valedictorian in 1929, had he not jumped out the 2nd story classroom window on a dare. The Principal of Rockhurst at the time, Father John Gerist, S.J., didn't approve of this behavior and made the decision that Bill Leahy would not be Valedictorian. Dad would always be known as smart, clever, a problem-solver, with a keen sense of humor and armed with a contagious laughter. From his early years, his parents and family called him "Hap" for Happy. Thus, it was my destiny! I would be educated in the Catholic tradition and breathe in the values enfolding me.

Mary Elizabeth Callahan was not allowed to wear a cap and gown at her high school graduation since she had been enrolled in the 3-year program.

My dad's graduation from Rockhurst High School, 1929.

Honor Students at Rockhurst High School, including Bill Leahy, my dad.

In 1950, our family moved to a larger home in the Brookside neighborhood. My parents realized the home on Troost was not big enough for a growing family. Besides, the Troost neighborhood was changing and becoming more commercial. Our new home was in a middle-class family-oriented neighborhood where children played outside from dawn until lightening bugs lit the yards. It was a mile from Visitation grade school and only 2 blocks from St. Teresa's Academy. I would spend the next 12 years of my life at those two schools. When the weather was good, I would walk the mile home from Visitation grade school always fearing those blocks where unleashed barking dogs could smell my fear. I wish someone had told me there were health benefits to walking. No one seemed to know this in the early 1950's or if they did the availability of cars seemed more attractive.

I was "a big girl for her age." Streetcar Conductors demanded a fare for me to ride as they believed my mother was lying when she told them I was under 7 years of age and could ride free. I loved playing jacks with friends and there were times when my mother would sit on the top step of our front porch and play jacks with me. It was at this time that Polio struck. Fear of Polio led to swimming pools closing and families being quarantined. I remember standing in long lines to get a Polio vaccine and the Tetanus shot when the industrial areas of Kansas City flooded in 1952. Although there were these health scares, these years were good. Our family seemed happy.

Martha is taller than her classmates in her Brownie Troop and at a birthday party.

Sister Olive Louise was my kindergarten teacher. She was a young nun, who had just taken her final vows with the Sisters of St. Joseph of Carondelet and been assigned to Saint Teresa's Academy and Visitation

Parish and grade school. There was a big clown's face painted on the rubber tiles of the kindergarten classroom floor. Before anyone could graduate from kindergarten, they had to be able to recite the ABC's forwards and backwards. Since I was a "big girl" for my age, I was expected to know these kinds of things. I met my first forever friend, Betsy Graham, in kindergarten. She was big like me. I mean she was tall like me but skinny like a fishing pole. I was lucky. My first experience with school was a good one. Sister Olive Louise liked me and often let me be Goldilocks when we played *Goldilocks and the Three Bears*.

Visitation grade school had an annual paper drive. The class that brought in the most papers won a fun day away from school, that included horseback riding at Benjamin Stables, a picnic that included roasted hot dogs on an open fire, ice cold soda pops (cream soda, orange, strawberry, and root beer) in clear glass bottles, ice cream bars and popsicles. Collecting Newspapers in the 50's was a way to raise money for charitable causes, and the paper drive funded Visitation grade school's need for educational resources. The kindergarten class had never won the paper drive in the 30 years of the school's history. However, Sister Olive Louise had a plan.

Sister Olive Louise called every kindergartner's home and asked the parents to help their child collect newspapers and magazines in their neighborhood. But the parents were cautioned not to tell anyone about the plan and most importantly, not to bring the papers to school until the very last morning of the paper drive. My mother and I went throughout the neighborhood pulling our well-used blue flyer wagon gathering papers and old magazines. As the paper drive progressed, the seventh graders were way ahead of the other classes and were already anticipating their celebratory party. (There were only 7 grades in the catholic schools in the early 1950's).

The morning of the last day of the paper drive, before the final weighing of the papers, every parent of every kindergartener showed up with a carload of papers. The piles of papers for the kindergarten class began to multiply. No other class even came close to kindergarten's "tons" of paper. The kindergarten class celebrated with Father Vincent Kearney. Sister Olive Louise not only understood the importance of education but how to engage others in her plans for success. She was a positive and competitive person. Later in her life, she would fundraise for her vision: Avila University. She became known in the community as the woman no one could say no, too. What a positive role model and influencer she was for me then and later in my life.

So much happens for the first time in a child's life between the ages of five and ten. For me it wasn't always as easy as kindergarten. In first grade I got into trouble for telling other children there was no Santa Claus. I fell under the merry-go-round where a large steel bolt holding the seats to the metal frame cut my head. I was treated at St. Luke's Emergency Room where they shaved part of my hair to put in stiches. I was also learning about other kinds of stitches. i.e., sewing and embroidering. My mom and I bought my first embroidery kit at the Brookside Dime Store, and I completed my first embroidered towels. Grandma Didi and mother sewed, and they were excited that I liked to sew as well.

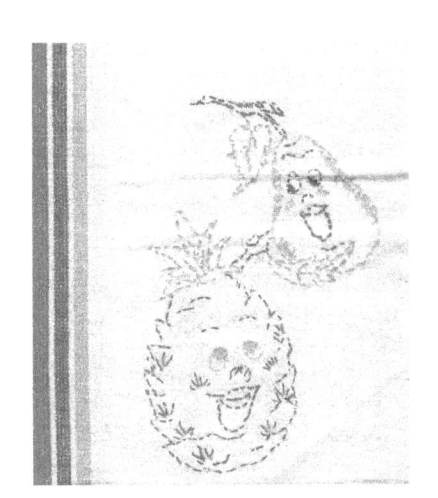

Martha's first attempt at embroidering kitchen towels

When I was five, my Aunt Tootsie, my dad's older sister, took me to lunch and to see the Fairy Princess at Kline's Department Store in downtown Kansas City, Missouri. The Fairy Princess was part of Kline's Christmas

Event for 35 years, between 1935 and 1970. The princess was beautiful, dressed in a long white sparkling dress with a tiara and holding a magic wand. When she waved the wand, a gift would suddenly appear on a circular moving belt. It just happened to be the gift I had told my aunt and the princess that I hoped to get.

One vivid memory I recall during this period of my life is from first grade. It was 1952, and I was 7 years old. One morning, my first-grade teacher, Sister Mary Ephram, CSJ, asked if there were students in the class who did not have a TV in their home. I remember looking around and hoping other children would raise their hands. My hand and one other hand went up slowly. This probably does not seem like a big deal, but it was for me. I remember this incident 70 years later. I never told anyone how this made me feel. I felt bad as my classmates looked at me. What was wrong with my family? Even at that young age of 7, I knew it was wrong to make some children feel less than other children. I never told my family how this experience or some other experiences made me feel. For some reason, I always thought I had to act like everything was okay. I'm not sure where that internal belief or sense came from.

I was tough on the playground. I thought everyone should play fair and get in line to go down the large metal twirling slide that was at least 15 feet high and burned my bottom when the sun was high. I fought with boys who pushed me out of the way so they could get in line ahead of me. I usually lost. In second grade, I had to stay after school because I didn't know how to spell "cat". I kept saying, "K-A-T." I'm not sure why Sister Ellen had to keep me after school, but I never forgot how to spell cat after that. Third grade was okay, except I began to realize there were birthday parties I wasn't invited to.

In fourth grade, I missed 56 days of school. I had frequent tonsillitis and swollen lymph nodes in my throat. I didn't understand it because I had had my tonsils removed when I was three years old. My older brother and sister were having their tonsils out at Menorah Medical Center in 1948, and the doctor thought my parents should save time and money by having my tonsils out as well. I guess doctors back then didn't understand that tonsils and adenoids can offer some defense to illnesses. By the time I was ten years old, my tonsils had grown back bigger and more troublesome. What happened next has had long term consequences. The doctor that was taking care of me recommended that I have my throat radiated rather than have another tonsillectomy. If you had acne or big tonsils back in the mid 50's, radiation was considered a treatment option. The health care system didn't fully understand the impact of radiation on the body. After multiple radiation treatments to my throat, I still had to have another tonsillectomy. During those many days at home, I looked through hundreds of magazines, memorized 15 verses of the Daniel Boone song, and turned every shoe box in the house into a shadow box using cutouts from cards and magazines. Despite those 56 days, I still passed 4th grade.

JULY 1955

Loose Park Summer Day Camp was a blessing. I attended it for two years, when I was 8 and 9 years old. Even though Loose Park was only 8 blocks from home my mother drove me there every morning. Rain or shine, the campers' day began with reciting "The Pledge of Allegiance." Days were filled with crafts, swimming lessons at Swope Park, hiking, and cookouts at Rocky Mountain campground in Swope Park. My favorite food over the campfire was squaw corn. It was made with kernels of corn, green onions, sweet and hot peppers, and tomatoes all stirred together over an open fire in a large, greased iron skillet. Most days, the Country Club Dairy truck would pull onto the grass near the Loose Park Tennis courts around noon and the man dressed in all white would leave a crate of milk and orange drink which we could purchase to have with the lunch we brought from home.

During my second year of camp, I became a Junior Leader, a title that meant I could help younger campers. I proudly attached my junior Leader badge to my self-made lanyard. Each day ended with singing TAPS, after which I ran to my mother's car for the short drive home.

I still remember and can sing our camp song, but I have no idea how to spell the words.

Chi-yai chi-yike-us
nobody like us
we are the kids from the Loose Park Camp
Always a winning,
always a grinning,
always a feeling fine.
Chi-yai!

Catholic families back in the 40's and 50's would gather in the evening to pray the rosary. Our family was no different. Every evening around 7 pm, no matter what we were doing, our family knelt in the upstairs hallway and said the rosary. The joyful, sorrowful, and glorious mysteries of the rosary were imprinted on my brain, and I can recite them to this day. The rosary ended with "Eternal rest grant unto them, O Lord, and let perpetual light shine upon them. May their souls and the souls of all the faithfully departed, through the mercy of God, rest in peace. Amen." Our ancestors were never forgotten, and my devotion to the Blessed Virgin Mary began early.

Habits are built early in one's life. Every Sunday I was expected to make the dessert for the "big meal." Following Mass and breakfast. I was to be in the kitchen by 10 am to start the pie dough from scratch or combine the cake mix with eggs and oil. I loved making pies because there was always left over dough. I would roll out the left-over dough and sprinkle lots of sugar and cinnamon on it with a few dots of butter. Then I would roll it up and bake it until the dough was crispy and the cinnamon and sugar oozed out its seam. This cinnamon roll was delicious. I learned to make Boston Crème pies, lemon pies, and banana coconut creme pies. I made angel food cakes for birthdays. My dad loved rice and tapioca puddings, and I made them especially for him. Baking has remained an important part of my life, and to this day I find myself in the kitchen when I have time in my schedule or when I'm confused, anxious, or troubled and don't know what to do. Even when money was short, I turned to the kitchen and made flourless cakes or silly cakes without eggs.

There were a lot of things I didn't understand at this age, and the fact that I didn't want others to know that I didn't know kept me quiet. I felt I should know more than I did, and therefore did not learn as much as I could. I have lots of examples of this. One afternoon when I was sitting on the white colonial sofa in our living room, I overheard my older sister talking to my mother in the kitchen about disc jockeys. I wondered how a disc jockey could ride a horse and play records at the same time. But I didn't ask. There was the time I overheard Dad tell Mom that his boss had fired someone. My dad and mom were upset. I couldn't help but think, "Isn't it a crime to kill someone?" Then there were the Sunday mornings after Mass when dad went to the bowling alley. Why would anyone want to throw a ball down a dark alley street, especially during the coldest months of the year? And, why in the world would anyone get dressed up to go to a wedding shower, when you were going to get wet? Or what about firebugs? If firebugs start fires, how come we can't get rid of them? But I didn't ask.

I don't know exactly how old I was before I learned that words don't mean the same things to everyone, and words can mean more than one thing. And for the longest time, I thought everyone thought like me. In fact, friends told me later in life that I acted like I knew everything, and that made them uncomfortable.

Major influencers and the lessons I was learning at this stage of my life:

Although I didn't understand everything being said at this age, there are three memories that I recall most often that influenced my life.

- Bang! With the wicks of the baby finger fireworks laced together it was easy to light one and then have 3 or 4 baby fingers go off. Bang, Bang, Bang! I was sitting on the top step in our front yard holding a lit punk and baby finger firecrackers. I was 7 years old and way too busy to notice the police officer who had stopped his car right in the middle of the street and walked toward me. No other family members were around. The officer told me it was against the law to shoot fireworks in the city. He told me to put them away and go into the house. I did just as he told me. He got back in his car and drove off. I went into the kitchen and told my mother what had happened. I don't remember what my mother's reaction was, just that nothing else happened or came from it.

I learned **there are laws,** and I need to follow them.

- My mother was pregnant, expecting Elizabeth Ann. She'd had an emergency C-section four years earlier when Michael Daniel was born prematurely due to placenta previa. Now, the doctor told her she would need to have another C-section and remain in the hospital for two weeks. According to my mother, our dad needed to work and there were no family members or friends that were willing to watch all four children, ages 4 through 12 years, for that length of time. After talking with a neighbor, Mrs. Barnard, my mom decided to place all four of us children temporarily in orphanages. My brothers went to the Boy's Orphans' Home on Westport Road, and my older sister and I went to St. Joseph's Girl's Orphanage at 31st and the Southwest Trafficway. Orphans were children we prayed for and collected money for at school and church. They were children who had no parents or families. At 7 years of age, I felt like an orphan.

My sister, Elizabeth Ann, was born on January 10th, 1952, a good two weeks after Christmas. To this day, I cannot understand why Christmas was celebrated at the orphanage in January. I remember having fried rabbit for Christmas dinner on a Friday evening and Santa coming and distributing gifts. My father visited and had dinner with me and my sister that evening. It was the only time I recall that anyone checked on us.

There was a large dorm room on the third floor of the orphanage's main building for girls my age. There was one long row of beds, like cots, down the middle of the room. Beds had to be made before breakfast and school. Rows and rows of new shoes were stored on rolling shelves nearby. One of the Sisters at the orphanage noticed that my shoes were worn and decided I needed a new pair of shoes. I chose the red Mary Jane shoes with a round toe and adjustable strap across the arch of my foot. I was told I could keep the shoes and take them home.

I attended first grade classes while I was there. First grade was in an adjacent building and the classroom was partly underground, like a basement. I never saw or spoke with my sister during this time. At least that's what I remember. Only decades later did I recall this experience. My sub-conscious did its thing by burying this experience deep in my mind. When I asked my sister about it years later, she thought being placed in the orphanage was "awful." Neither she nor I had told anyone about the experience. It was traumatic for sure. I do not remember even one child I met there.

I learned that **Family is important. Care for one another**. Some children don't have a family.

- I stayed with Grandma Didi throughout my early years. Her home was small. There was a cozy front room, dining room, 2 bedrooms (one in the front of the house and one in the back of the house), a bathroom with a tub and toilet, a kitchen with a wood burning stove and an unheated add-on back porch, rightfully called the refrigerator or steam room depending on the season. She lived just north of the Country Club Plaza on top of a hill. One day while Grandma Didi was rocking in her favorite chair and I was sitting near her on the floor, she said, "Martha, make your hay while the sun shines." I wasn't sure what she meant. She continued to tell me that my best years would be my teenage years, and I needed to take advantage of them. Grandma was seventeen when she came to America. "Make your hay while the sun shines" meant for grandma Didi, meet a young man, marry, and have children at a young age. "Life gets harder the older you get," she said. Grandma wanted better for me.

I learned there are **developmental milestones and expectations associated with them.**

I was also learning at this time:

Competition is fun and when you win you get rewarded.

Don't single people out and make them feel bad – **be thoughtful and consider how others might feel.**

Ask questions when you don't understand something.

Words can mean more than one thing.

Cooking is fun, and I love to eat what I made.

How to pray and especially the importance of prayer to the Blessed Virgin Mary.

I liked being a junior camp leader who helped younger campers complete projects.

The reader's most significant memories and influencers from five to ten years of age.

Chapter 3

1955 to 1960

Martha: 10 to 15 Years of Age

I ATTENDED VISITATION grade school from kindergarten through eighth grade. I was liked by most of my classmates, but I was no one's best friend. I had trouble making small talk and still do. I wore size 9 shoes and lived within a 5'9" frame. I was physically healthy but emotionally self-conscious and insecure. I felt like a giant around my friends. My mother was constantly telling me to stand up straight. I wish someone had told me that being tall and thin was a good thing and those big feet would carry me through the exciting journey ahead.

I was 12 years old and in 6th grade when the Catholic Diocese of Kansas City-St. Joseph, responsible for the catholic schools in Kansas City, Missouri, decided to add an 8th grade to their grade schools. My classmates and I were told we would take an exam to determine our class placement for the coming year. The 6th grade students who scored in the top half on the exam would skip ahead and move to the newly established 8th grade. The 6th grade students that scored in the bottom half on the exam would continue to 7th grade.

The 7th grade class was split the same way. Students in 7th grade who scored in the top half of their class on the exam graduated and went on to high school. The students who scored in the bottom half on the exam would join the upper half of the 6th grade to form the 8th grade. I scored well enough to skip 7th grade and move up to 8th grade. For me it was a positive life experience. However, this method for determining how to create an eighth grade had a lifelong negative impact on those students who had to stay behind. It is not too strong a statement to say some suffered post-traumatic stress syndrome. Most of my close friends moved up to eighth grade with me, including Betsy.

Back in the 50's, grade school students lined up to do everything. There was a line to go out for recess. There was a line for the drinking fountain. There was a line to go to the bathroom. There was a line for processing to and from church. The shortest students were always first in line followed by students incrementally by height. Boys were always first in line, followed by the girls. Betsy and I were always partners and the last in line. If Betsy was sick, I would have to walk alone at the end of the line. All eyes were on me, the last, the biggest in my class.

I started drinking coffee in 6th grade. Mother had small ceramic mugs in which she would pour coffee and then add a splash of milk for me to enjoy prior to leaving for school. I loved coffee then and still do. Now I even understand it's good for you. I'm evidence that coffee does not stunt one's growth.

Monsignor Arthur M. Tighe, a priest wide as he was tall, became the Pastor of Visitation church and school in 1957. He was Irish and had a booming authoritarian voice that silenced everything and everyone around him. On stormy Friday afternoons he visited the 8th grade classroom and told us ghost stories. The stories carried over three or four class periods, leaving us clinging to our desks and begging for more. It was a wonderful year.

At the end of my 8th grade year, I was voted May Queen by my classmates. The May Queen places a crown of flowers on the Blessed Virgin Mary's statue during the annual May Day procession. I wore a beautiful white organdy dress loaned to me by Judy Schloegel and her mother. Judy had worn the dress the year before, as May Queen. My mother was there with my younger sister. Looking back, I do not remember my father being at the May Crowning or at many of the special moments in my life. As a parent, and even now as a grandparent, I wouldn't miss a recital, a confirmation, or a sporting event, of my children or grandchildren unless I was ill or out of town. Part of this is that we live in a different time, but it makes me sad to recall his absence. I do remember attending the father-daughter dance at STA with my dad. It was awkward. We did not have much to talk about

In 1958, Martha was the May Queen in 8th grade at Visitation Catholic church. She is surrounded by her attendants and her brother, Michael, and her sister, Elizabeth.

When Dad was younger, he did all sorts of projects around our home. I remember him painting our big old two-story house using multiple stepladders that had to be held in place by me and my siblings, especially when he painted under the eaves. Since dad usually worked 5 ½ days a week my mother and older brother usually cared for the yard.

On Saturday's, Mother loved to go downtown shopping. After finding a parking space our first stop was always the Jones Department Store, at the southeast corner of 12th and Main Street. The Jones Department Store is where Mother would consult with a cosmetologist who advised her on face cream and other beauty products. Depending on what we were looking for we would then visit Kline's and Emery-Bird-Thayer. We always walked past Harzfeld's department store located on Petticoat Lane to admire the window dressings but seldom entered such an expensive store. Mostly, we ate lunch at Kresge's, a five and dime store, where you usually stood to eat a chili dog and drink root beer from a large, frosted mug. The eating area was small, with only six stools on which to sit, and they were always filled.

On occasion we ate at Wolferman's located at 1108 Walnut. Wolferman's, which was famous for its English muffins and chicken salad, opened originally in 1888 and then moved to the Walnut location in 1895. Sometimes we ate at The Forum cafeteria, where I always ordered chicken pot pie. My favorite restaurant was the Italian Gardens where I ordered a cheese pizza. I can still taste and smell their pizza. I think there were some secret ingredients on top of the cheese, maybe thyme and rosemary, that no other Italian restaurant has ever been able to duplicate for me. (As I was going through some old silverware of my mother's I found several forks engraved Forum.)

During our summer vacations in 1957 and 1958, we spent time at Silver Moon Resort on the Lake of the Ozarks near Gravois Mills, Missouri. Grandma and Grandpa Callahan traveled with us to the lake. Dad stayed home to work. Grandma usually sat outside on the porch of the old stone home we rented, only moving to prepare meals. Grandma Didi had stomach cancer in 1954 and never fully recovered from the surgical gastric resection that removed the tumor. Most days, she and my mother fixed fried chicken, potato salad, and slaw. There was always cake, ice cream and watermelon. I never missed a meal growing up.

While at the lake, Grandpa would get up by 6 or 7 am and head for the floating fishing shack which was secured by cables to an old stone wall. There was a hole in the middle of the floor, where you could fish regardless of the weather. He caught mostly crappie which he threw back into the lake complaining that he wouldn't waste his time frying them up.

Silver Moon was a family resort. We spent all day jumping into the lake off a floating boat dock, playing badminton, and eating. I always had on my orange life jacket since I really didn't know how to swim. We rented the original resort owner's home the first year but stayed in the two-story lodge the following year. It's the second season there that is most memorable. We stayed on the upper floor of the lodge in the apartment farthest from the stairs. One evening while mother was preparing dinner, she struck a match to light the oven's gas pilot. At just that moment, the rotating fan close by blew the flame, catching my mother's hair on fire and singeing her eyebrows and eyelashes. Mother yelled for help. I don't remember exactly what happened next, but I do remember her hair being burnt on the ends, her brows curling, and her eyelashes turning light orange. That was our last trip to Silver Moon, not because we didn't want to go back, but because the manager suggested that we might like to find somewhere else to stay the following year.

I grew up sharing a bedroom and a double bed with my older sister. The bed got smaller with each of our birthdays, and once Mary Helen started dating (she was 5 years older than me) I was often woken at midnight or 1:00 am when my sister got home. There was a good side to sharing the small bedroom. Mary Helen had a portable Hi-Fi record player and bought long playing 33 1/3 albums of the current musicals: Oklahoma, My Fair Lady, The King and I, Carousel, etc. Music played throughout our bedroom every waking hour. I memorized every song in every musical. With no air conditioning in the 50's, all the neighbors had their windows open and knew I loved to sing.

I was only 13 when I entered high school, and the next four years passed quickly. I always liked the August tradition of preparing for a new school year. I usually chose black and white laced oxford (saddle) shoes because of the way they looked on other students' feet. My uniform was a white short sleeved blouse under a powder blue, maroon, or mustard gold jumper. Black and gold were the school colors. I savored the new tablets and binders, promising myself things would be better this year, and I would stay more organized.

High School was one of the worst times of my life and one of the best times of my life. I didn't feel like I had any control over my body or life. My body was changing, and I had no one to talk to about it. I did not know what I didn't know. I was naïve. Everyone at school talked to me, but no one ever shared secrets or gossip with me. Years later I learned who got pregnant in my high school class. Scholastically, I learned mostly through rote memory and could pass tests, but really didn't retain much knowledge those first few years. I wish I had understood the importance of my Civics class back then. Only now, 50 years later, have I realized that others in my class were having the same feelings and thoughts.

As a Junior and Senior, I developed some lifelong friendships and began to work harder to make good grades. My mother had me take private voice lessons after a short and unproductive stint of dance lessons. I engaged in extra-curricular activities. Attending an all-girls' Catholic high school offered me opportunities to take on leadership roles. I worked on the yearbook. I was a member of the Sodality and Latin clubs. I found my voice, literally and figuratively. I liked singing and performing in school plays and class competitions. Although I was not destined to be a singer, the three years of private voice lessons and recitals prepped me to be more self-assured and more confident as a future public speaker and educator.

My parents never encouraged me to excel in school. There are fewer expectations expressed for a middle child, not out of neglect, but because parents are busy with the issues of the oldest and youngest child. Don't misunderstand me, I think that it was beneficial. My parents once told me that they didn't push me because they knew I already wanted to succeed at whatever I was doing. My girlfriends still call me competitive.

It was late summer of 1957, when our family took a trip to Chicago, Illinois. My dad worked for a grain company located within the Kansas City Board of Trade Building. Dad was interested in showing us the trading floor in the Board of Trade Building in Chicago. It was kind of like being in New York and visiting the New York Stock Exchange building. Mother planned the trip to Chicago concerning herself with the details. She wrote multiple hotels in downtown Chicago near the train depot and asked how much it would cost for a family of 7 to stay in the hotel for one week. She made a reservation at the hotel that offered our family the lowest rate. The train to Chicago had an observation car and dining car. It was only an eight-hour train ride but Mother brought sacks of food even though we had reservations to eat in the formal dining car, where men in white jackets and white gloves took our orders and served us on white linen tablecloths with real silver utensils.

Once we arrived at Chicago Union Station, we each carried our own suitcase to the Hotel, approximately one mile away. Mother, who managed the money in our home, wouldn't waste money on a taxi. In the 50's there were no such thing as suitcases with wheels, so we each struggled carrying a heavy case filled with a week's worth of clothes down Michigan Avenue.

What we must have looked like entering the Palmer House Hotel on Monroe and Wabash streets, I can only imagine. The only comparison I can make is that of Jed Clampett and his family moving from the Ozark Hills to Beverly Hills.

In the 1950's, the Palmer House could be compared to today's Hotel Continental or the Ritz Carlton. When Dad tried to check us into the hotel there was a problem. Dad called mom up to the desk and asked her to show the receptionist her letter of confirmation. The letter was on Palmer House stationery and clearly stated that the Leahy family of 7 could stay at the Palmer House for one week for $27.00 a night. The receptionist explained that there had been a typographical mistake. The confirmation should have read $127.00 per night. Words were exchanged at the desk, but after what seemed like a long time, we were escorted to our hotel room on the 2nd floor. It was a ginormous room with one double bed in the corner and a single bathroom with tub. Five cots were rolled in and lined up, one for each child. Also in the room were white dressing tables with mirrors and each had a small spinning stool to sit on. For what else? Trying on hats! The room was a millinery sales room where hats were sold to retailers. Hats were everywhere. My mom, sisters and I had fun trying on all the hats. I came home with a red feather cloche. Seven of us had stayed at one of the most beautiful hotels in all of Chicago, for $27.00 a night.

We dined at George Diamond Steak House, where I was introduced to a wedge salad with blue cheese dressing for the first time. It was delicious. We visited Lincoln Park Zoo, the Museum of Science and Industry, Riverview Amusement Park, Lake Michigan, and the tallest building in Chicago, the Prudential building. Of course, there was also the body in the alley, and the man who pick pocketed another on the city bus and then threw the wallet at my dad when he came close to being caught.

One of my favorite memories is my dad agreeing to take me on the parachute ride at Riverview Amusement Park. We sat in a small seat with safety restraints and were pulled up in the air several hundred feet. When we reached the top, the parachute was released, and we floated down.

Somehow there were ropes or wires that prevented us from blowing away. Only when the ride was over could I say, "it was fun."

My parents went on a date one night in Chicago and left the 5 of us kids alone in the hotel millinery salesroom. They went to the Empire Room off the first floor of the hotel for drinks, dancing, and to listen to Hildegard. The Empire Room was famous for hosting some of the best entertainers in the country, like Frank Sinatra, Judy Garland, Ella Fitzgerald, and Louis Armstrong. It is one of the only times I recall my parents going on a date. It made me happy to see them happy.

Some Sundays during the summer my family and grandparents, Didi and the Mick, would drive to Excelsior Springs, Missouri to swim in the public pool, have a picnic, and then visit the Hall of Waters where grandma Didi would buy special waters to help settle her stomach.

After my Grandma Didi died the summer of 1959, things were never the same at home. That summer we took grandpa, via the railroad, to New Orleans to help him through the loss of Didi, but as it turned out, we all missed Didi not being with us. Her death changed my mother. Mother had lost her best friend.

Major influencers and the lessons I was learning at this stage of my life:

During this period of my life, I continued to cope with the changes in my body. The world was getting bigger and more unknown to me. Yet, it is these three critical events/ memories that I still think about seven decades later.

- I took my first train ride in 1956, when I was eleven years old. Our family was headed to Saint Louis. My siblings and I were so excited we barely sat down. We visited the snack bar in the next train car repeatedly. Looking back others on the train must have thought we were walking to St. Louis or maybe eating our way to St. Louis. Grandpa had worked most of his life for the GM&O Railroad and was able to get us reduced and or free fares. I worked for days preparing for this trip. I remember making a beige and lime green skirt for the trip and spending time ironing my clothes and packing them neatly in a suitcase. It was going to be an adventure. After a few hours, we arrived at the train depot in Saint Louis. I don't remember much about the trip or where we stayed or what we did. I only remember being disappointed. St. Louis looked just like Kansas City. I was anticipating a city that looked different, better, bigger, and more fun. Why travel to a city that looks just like Kansas City?

I learned that what you imagine a place will be like is not always the way it is. **Read and learn** about other places before you visit them.

- Mrs. Martin was my 5th grade teacher. She was also the best teacher I had in grade school. She was the first teacher that took a personal interest in me. She told my mother that I needed to attend summer school to strengthen my reading skills. So that summer I attended summer school at Saint Elizabeth's Catholic grade school. Summer school had a profound impact on me. I remember the first two books I read that summer: a mystery called "Bramble

Bush" and the "Story of Marco Polo". I cannot tell you who the authors were, but I loved both books and began to enjoy reading. Although I had a library card and went to the library every two weeks in the summer from a young age, I usually skimmed the books and read the pictures. I do not remember anyone ever reading to me as a young child and no one wanted to listen to me read out loud.

I learned **to love reading** and I understood that my teacher **cared about me** and wanted to help me get better at reading.

- My first high school report card arrived in the mail from Saint Teresa's Academy. I opened it and looked at my grades. I was excited and ran to show my mom, who was outside raking the front yard. She didn't react. Rather, she said. "I knew you would do well. You give 100% to everything you do." That was it. I put the card away disappointed that she didn't hug me, and cheer! I needed to hear that she was proud of me. Of course, we never were a hugging family. It wasn't the experience that day but the foundation that was set: I could do what I put my mind to.

I learned that **it is important to recognize one's achievements and celebrate with them** and encourage them to continue doing good work. Let them know how proud you are of them.

I was also learning at this time:

I liked getting **good grades** and was proud of my accomplishments. Others may not realize how important success was to me.

Mother was very **thrifty,** and it was important to hold on to documents that reflect your understanding of agreements.

Smiling is good and people are happy when I smile.

Life changes when someone you love dies.

Singing is fun and I like to sing.

The Reader's most significant memories and influences from 10 to 15 years of age:

My Grandparents as Influencers

I BRIEFLY DIGRESS from my life timeline to tell you about my grandparents. It is important to understand that my grandparents' and parents' life experiences stitched together the environment that embraced me. I learned their ways. I listened to their ideologies. Even though I rebelled in some ways, the way I was raised continued to influence me throughout my life. I was the third of five grandchildren and a second-generation child born in America.

My maternal grandmother, Didi, was born in Rostrevor, County Down, Ireland, on October 10th, 1886. I was named for Grandma Didi, who was christened Bridget Morgan.

Grandma Didi's parents, Mary Morris and James Morgan, both born around 1851, were Catholic. Grandma was the third of six children and given the baptismal name of Bridget. She had two older siblings: Elizabeth (Lizzie) and Peter. She had three younger siblings: James (Jimmy), Mary, and Rose.

Northern Ireland was then and is now governed by The Church of England. Catholics were subject to the Monarchy and remained the working class for the wealthy. Catholics in Northern Ireland experienced centuries of oppression by the English and all attempts by the Irish to gain Independence failed. The young in Ireland yearned to be free and believed they could have a better life if they migrated to the United States.

Life in Ireland had not been easy for Bridget. When grandma finished third grade she went to work. She was hired, three months at a time, to care for children and prepare dinners for protestant, Anglican families. She earned fifty cents for three months labor. Grandma would not return home for weeks at a time, but when she did, she gave the fifty cents she had earned to her parents so they could pay their mortgage and "keep" the family farm.

Growing up in Northern Ireland was hard for a young catholic girl. Out of necessity, grandma Didi learned to sew, darn socks, and repair and resole her shoes, all skills she brought to America with her. She cut up worn out clothes to make bedspreads and quilts.

When word came one day that her mother was sick, Bridget raced home and saw her mother, Mary Morris Morgan, lying beneath a tree having difficulty breathing. Her mother died August 4th, 1896 from Influenza at 49 years of age. It was only two years later, March 30th, 1898 that Bridget's father, James Morgan, died at the age of 55 from influenza and pneumonia. After their father's death the six children decided to sell the family farm and split the money. Five of the children used the money to come to America while Lizzie and her husband moved to Liverpool, England. The Morgan children wanted to escape poverty and the hardship of Northern Ireland. The Morgan home and property was sold and has since been owned by Arthur Quinn and is currently owned by Kieraim Morgan.

Didi arrived, alone, at Ellis Island in 1903 at the age of 17. When she saw the Statue of Liberty she said it was the most beautiful thing she had ever seen. The voyage to the U.S. was not easy. Didi had purchased a ticket stamped Steerage: 3rd class. In the late 19th and early 20th centuries steamship steerage decks were used to provide the lowest cost and lowest class of travel. Didi was happy she had an upper bunk on the ship and Didi was never allowed above deck to smell or taste the fresh air, but her dreams for America assuaged any regrets she might have had leaving Ireland.

When Didi arrived in the United States the Immigration Authority at Ellis Island changed her name from Bridget Morgan to Delia Morgan. I'm not sure why or with what authority they did this. Some say there were just too many Bridget's coming into the U.S. from Ireland, while oral history suggests that the name Bridget translated to the American name of Delia.

To enter the United States of America during the early 1900s, you had to be in good health, have a confirmed place of employment, and at least $25.00. Grandma's older brother, Peter, was already in Kansas City and had arranged for grandma to have a job as a domestic with the J.R. Kelly Family at 33rd and Main Street. The Kelly's were a well-to-do family that owned the Kelly Cooperage Plant in Armourdale at Shawnee Avenue and Brent Street. They built barrels for flour, fruit, vinegar, pork, and lard, and kegs for liquor. Mrs. Kelly took a liking to Didi and took time to teach her about American life. Grandma always had positive stories to tell about her time with the Kelly family and how that experience bolstered her self-confidence.

Pictures of the home where Grandma, her parents, and her five-siblings lived are on the following pages." It was on a small plot of land they called the farm. Initially it was one room with dirt floors and when it rained, mud flowed downhill into their home. Later a second room was added. An outdoor area was used for cooking when the weather allowed. Rocks restricted the soil and made it impossible to grow crops. The family had come by the property as the British government, to appease the working class and de-escalate the fighting between Catholics and Protestants, allowed each Irish family to buy a vertical slice of farmland from the government, which they could pay for over time. Although rocky and unable to produce crops, the Morgan property offered a view of the Carlingford Lough and the beautiful green hills of Ireland, striped with stone hedges.

Grandma Didi's home in Rostrevor, County Down, Northern Ireland.

Grandma Didi experienced loss and emotional pain throughout her life. Besides losing both of her parents before the age of seventeen, three of her siblings died young and unexpectedly, and two of them distanced themselves from her. Her greatest loss came later in life when grandma's first child and only son, Daniel James, died unexpectedly at the age of 18. (See Appendix A for additional information on Bridget "Didi" Morgan's family.)

Grandma's eyes were light blue, almost transparent, like a bright sky in the early morning. She had a notched nose, some call a Roman nose, that was characteristic of Coit Morgan's. Her long thinning hair, the color of sweet corn, was always pulled back from her face and rolled up and held in place with hair pins and a hair switch made from mutton. Her legs, thick and log-like, were usually covered by heavy tan colored cotton opaque hose held up by elastic garters placed below her knees. In the summer months I'd see her café-au-lait birthmark on her left leg and as she got older and lost weight due to cancer, her dentures clicked when she spoke.

Grandma liked to talk in aphorisms: "Early to bed and early to rise makes you healthy, wealthy, and wise." "A bird in the hand is worth two in the bush." If you dropped your fork at the dinner table, Grandma was sure to say, "Company is coming" from the north, south, east, or west, depending on how the tongs of the fork pointed. Or if someone had big ears, she would say that's a good trait to have. People with big ears are generous. And lord knows if you found your ears burning, someone was talking about you. And "Never look a gift horse in the mouth." If you were not feeling well, it was because, "You are burning the candle at both ends." Grandma cooked on a wood burning stove until her death, making biscuits and corn bread with butter and jam that melted in your mouth. Her unpeeled boiled potatoes were poured onto the kitchen table for us to pick up and put on our plates.

Grandma lived two blocks from the Country Club Plaza shopping area in a small home. The garage was converted into a chicken coop. When I spent the night with her, I'd collect warm eggs in the morning, careful to avoid the chicken poop that was everywhere. She sold chickens by the pound and eggs by the half dozen. She buried aluminum cans and the ashes from the wood burning stove in the back yard, telling me that the soil was good to us, and we had to give back to the soil. She loved flowers. During the winter months her dining room table was covered with green plants nourished by the sun pouring in the east dining room window. In the summer months her yard smelled of peonies and roses with a large Holly bush abutting the front porch where she would occasionally sit.

She was always busy and seldom sat down. She woke every morning at 5:30 am and walked a mile to Guardian Angels Catholic Church to attend daily mass. She did this come rain, snow, or sleet and never missed daily mass after her son, Danny, died. She mostly walked in the grass to save her shoe leather, always keeping her head down hoping to find loose change someone might have dropped in the curb or on the grass. The fear of poverty was ever present, overarching and restricting her life and decisions. Grandma fixed dinner at noon or one o'clock since Grandpa needed a big meal before he left for work, the three to midnight shift. Supper was a light meal at six in the evening.

I loved sharing Christmas Day with Grandma and Grandpa. The day started early. My mom, brothers and sisters and I would rise by 5:00 am, dress, and hurry to the car to pick up grandma for 6:00 am mass at Our Lady of Good Counsel Catholic Church. We were cautioned not to look in the living room under the Christmas tree as we exited the front door. Grandpa didn't come to mass with us. He had worked to the wee hours of the morning and slept in. More than likely, he caught midnight mass on his way home from work. Mass at 6:00 am was fast and over within 25 to 30 minutes due to the short biblical readings, the absence of a homily, and the few in attendance receiving Holy Communion. After taking Grandma back home we would race home to open presents. I loved this tradition because it made Christmas Day last longer. Around 9:00 or 10:00 am, after my dad had been to mass, we would drive over to my grandparents' home to bring them to our home for the day. As soon as we arrived at Grandma's and Grandpa's, my dad was invited into the kitchen for a "Hot Toddy." That must have been a traditional start to Christmas day in Ireland.

If I spent the night with Grandma, she cared for me as she had the Protestant families' children in Northern Ireland. I had a bath at 5 pm, dressed in clean clothes, had supper, and went to bed by 7 pm after saying my prayers, even in the summer. I shared the bath water with my siblings when they were with me. In the morning, I would rise by 6 am and dress in the clean clothes I had put on for supper the evening before.

Grandma had a large walk-in closet in her bedroom and when it stormed and I was with her, we went into the closet and sat on the floor. Her fear of thunderstorms came from the time lightning entered through the front door of her home and existed out the back window. Once Grandma closed the closet door the lightning stopped and thunder softened. I could see grandma Didi's fingers move along the rosary beads in her hands and hear her soft voice, "Hail Mary, full of grace...." Wrapped and twisted around grandma's neck were two or three scapulars of the Sacred Heart of Jesus, the Blessed Mother, and the Holy Family. I never fell asleep in the closet because once Grandma completed the rosary, she would retell the stories she brought with her to America from the north of Ireland. She repeated the story about her sister, Mary, who was kidnapped by the "Little People" in Ireland and kept for three days. When Mary came home, she could not remember anything about where she had been. Grandma often told the stories of how the parents of the children she cared for in Northern Ireland were demanding and mean to her.

Grandma told me *she* proposed to Grandpa. She said to Grandpa, "As long as you are going to keep coming around here, we might as well get married." I have Grandma's wedding rings, which I only saw her wear on special occasions. She told me her hands were for working. Since Grandpa could not afford an engagement ring, Grandma offered to use the one another boyfriend had given her, and grandpa bought her a gold wedding band at a local pawn shop with someone else's initials etched inside. She and my grandfather, Michael Daniel O'Callaghan, his name also changed by the Immigration Authority at Ellis Island to Callahan, married on September 22nd, 1909, at Redemptorist Catholic Church in Kansas City, Missouri and were married a few months short of their 50th wedding anniversary. They had two children: Daniel (Danny) James (1910) and Mary Elizabeth (1914). Grandpa had applied and became a citizen of the United States, and once Grandma married Grandpa, she automatically became a U.S. citizen. I treasure Grandma's rings and wear them most days.

What outsiders never knew is that Grandma Didi left a rich legacy to her only surviving child, a daughter, my mother, Mary Elizabeth. My mother was named after Grandma's two sisters that died: Lizzie (Elizabeth) and Mary. Grandma, who cleaned people's homes, cared for their children, and served dinner to members of the Mission Hills Country Club, saved her money, and never spent a penny on "foolishness." She learned how to buy second and third mortgages during and after the depression. A lawyer by the name of Isadorf helped grandma buy the properties. She hid the money she earned in her home, under the bed, in the mattress, and places others wouldn't find it. Before her death, she deposited her money in the Columbia National Bank with the help of her lawyer, George Aylward. Oral history records that the Bank officers were upset when Grandma walked in with so much cash, and Mr. Brown questioned where all the money had come from. Mr. Aylward told them to mind their own business.

I was 14 when Grandma Didi died in 1959 at the age of 73 from bone and stomach cancers. She died at home in her own bed. Before she died, she made one request of my mother and my brother, Bill, who was with her. Grandma Didi said, "Tell the Mick (my grandfather) and others how successful I was." Grandma had achieved her dream. She had worked hard and saved her money. She was never poor in the United States of America. She never asked for anything other than a better, secure future for herself and family.

Grandma's financial resources and savings helped her grandchildren attend the best Catholic schools in Kansas City. Eight years after her death, in 1967, my brother, Bill, was cleaning out the coal bin in the basement of grandma's home. There he found an overlooked mason jar of money, mostly small bills, totaling $1900. The money was bundled with a shoestring holding the bills in place.

In July of 2022, the money was passed by my brother, Bill, to me. Only $900 of the money remains, as part of it was given to my younger sister, Elizabeth Ann, years ago to take a ski trip to Winter Park, Colorado, with her high school friends. Mother went with her.

More important than money, grandma left a legacy of hard work. She taught my mother survival skills: how to cook, how to hang wallpaper, how to paint, how to sew, how to darn, and most importantly how to save money and avoid debt. Didi was a businesswoman. She was tough, strong, and someone who fought for what she believed in. She owned properties throughout Kansas City till the 1950's. She owned homes in the Valentine shopping center, along 44th and Bellevue Street, and at 50th & Main Street in Kansas City, Missouri. She sold the properties after my dad, an accountant, told her she could get into trouble for not paying taxes on the properties. Grandma clearly valued hard work, her faith, family, and being self-sufficient. She did not want to be dependent on others.

Grandma was strong-minded, determined, persistent, and was willing to fight for what she thought was right. Grandma was also stubborn. I loved Didi.

My Maternal Grandfather, Michael Daniel O'Callaghan was born July 2, 1881, in County Claire, Ireland, in the town of Inagh, located in the southwest part of Ireland, near Ennis and south of the Cliffs of Mohr. Grandpa Callahan, called "The Mick" because of his size, was the first child born to Daniel O'Callaghan and Nora Casey. His mother, Nora, died during childbirth with her sixth child. His dad, Daniel, married Bridget Gallagher several years later and had nine more children. Grandpa had five siblings and nine stepbrothers and stepsisters. Grandpa worked with his dad at the family-owned rock quarry. They mined rock for the construction of roads, bridges, and homes. Grandpa left school after 6th grade, as reflected on his school attendance records and logs.

Oral history recalls that Bridget Gallagher, the stepmother, was a mean woman. She would hit the children when they didn't do what they were told. One day, my grandfather, who was 16 at the time, had had enough. He told his stepmother that if she ever hit his sisters again, he was going to beat her up. The stepmother warned him that when his father got home, he was going to "beat the shit out of him." Knowing this would happen Grandpa packed his few belongings and left his home in Inagh. (See Appendix B for additional information on Michael Daniel Callahan's life.)

> IN LOVING MEMORY OF
> DANIEL CALLAGHAN
> *SHANAVALLA,*
> DIED 1912
> HIS WIFE NORA *NEE* CASEY
> DIED 1892
> DANIEL JNR.
> DIED 1930
> REST IN PEACE
> ERECTED BY THE FAMILY

It's interesting to note that Daniel O'Callaghan, my great grandfather, is buried in Inagh next to his first wife, Nora, and the tombstone reflects Daniel's life and only that of his first wife, Nora.

After grandpa left his home, he made his way to Liverpool, England where he boarded a ship to New York, landing at Ellis Island in 1901. After coming to the United States, Grandpa started out in Massachusetts, but gradually worked his way to Iowa where an older couple that had no children of their own employed him. After a few years, grandpa realized he did not want to continue farming and headed to Kansas City. The older couple tried to persuade him to stay in Iowa by promising to leave him the farm upon their death, but his mind was made up. He was 22 years old and wanted to move to the city. Besides, he had relatives, including his aunt Nellie O'Callaghan and aunt Bridget O'Callaghan Logan in Kansas City. Family was important to him.

Once in Kansas City, Grandpa was immediately hired as a streetcar conductor. Back in the early 1900's, the streetcar was a covered wagon pulled by horses. Grandpa tried driving the horses, but management decided he was better at collecting the money at the back of the wagon. Shortly thereafter, he met my grandma Didi who introduced him to Mrs. J. R. Kelly. Grandpa then went to work at Kelly Cooperage, making all kinds of barrels and kegs.

Michael Daniel O'Callaghan and Bridget (Delia) Morgan married on September 22, 1909. They had two children, Daniel James and Mary Elizabeth.

Clockwise from top left, Grandpa fishing at Loose Park; Grandpa and Grandma Didi with their daughter Mary Elizabeth, and grandchildren, Billy, Martha, and Mary Helen; Grandma Didi and grandpa as they aged; Grandpa at his retirement party from GM&O railroad in 1957.

Grandpa spent most of his life working for the railroad, jumping box cars and chasing drifters who stole their way onto the train. Grandpa saw his share of fights. As a Special Agent, Grandpa worked for the Chicago & Alton (Illinois) line that became the Chicago & Baltimore line, that became the Baltimore & Ohio (B&O) line, and that finally became the Gulf, Mobile, & Ohio line (GM&O).

Working for the railroad meant Grandpa walked at least 26 miles a day, 8 miles from his home to his job in the West Bottoms of Kansas City and 8 miles back home. Then another 10 or 20 miles during his shift providing security to the railroad. He worked six days a week, 9 to 12 hours a day, from 3 pm till midnight or later. Prior to going to work Grandpa often sat at the kitchen table, (a table with a big round belly drawer where potatoes and other vegetables were stored for long periods of time) and opened a tin of sardines, still with their heads and swimming in oil. He'd make sardine sandwiches that included thick slices of onion and garlic packed between two slices of Irish soda bread. He sometimes complained that his stomach hurt but charcoal tablets would relieve the discomfort.

Grandpa always greeted me the same way. "Top of the morning to ye." As a child, I often sat on Grandpa's big iron bed, painted white with raw metal peeking through the chipped paint, and watch him prepare to go to work. Grandpa and Grandma each had their own bedrooms so as not to wake each other with their disparate daily schedules. Grandpa would put on a three-piece suit to hide what was underneath. He laced up his high-top boots. He'd attach his blackjack to his belt and strap on his shoulder holster and gun. It was kind of like watching a TV western with the good guy getting ready to confront the bad guy in town. He never let me or my siblings hold his gun, or even the bullets. He was hurt more than a few times and retired with distinction at the age of 76, in 1957.

My grandparents valued faith, family, and hard work. Neither wanted to return to Ireland as thoughts of Ireland brought forth painful memories. They came to America so they could have a better life for themselves, their children, and grandchildren. I never observed any affection exchanged between my grandparents, nor conversations. They spoke to each other in words, not sentences, seemingly understanding each other. Of course, they were older when I knew them but I don't think they ever recovered from the pain of losing their son, Daniel James, the loss of family, and fear of poverty. (See Appendix C for information about Danny Callahan.)

Grandpa's diversion from work was fishing or sitting in his rocking chair with a pipe in his mouth listening to a ballgame being broadcast on the radio, a can of beer nearby. His old chair transports me now as I rock in the living room of my home. Grandpa died May 24, 1971. Growing up grandpa had spent part of each day fishing in the Lough Inagh Lake near his home. He told me sometimes he went to the Cliffs of Mohr to fish. In Kansas City, I saw him more than once fishing at Loose Park Lake.

My Paternal Grandparents were Mary Magdalene (Mamie) Foley Leahy (1879-1952) and William (Billy) James Leahy, Jr. (Born January 30, 1872 and died on January 17th, 1938). I know little about my paternal grandparents. My father's mother, Mary Magdalene Foley, or Mamie as she was known, died at the age of 73 when I was 7 years old. She was born in 1879 to Timothy Foley and Elizabeth Ryan. According to her death certificate, she died of congestive heart failure. Those who knew her said she was a beautiful, smart, and classy woman. She was a great cook, and everyone loved her potato salad. I remember she was big busted. Her busts or bosoms were not where they were supposed to be but rather laid on her abdomen. She loved to have fun and play jokes on people. One Fourth of July she scared me and my family by throwing lit firecrackers from our front porch onto the lawn while in a wheelchair. We had no idea where she got the firecrackers, or the lighter.

My dad's father, Billy Leahy, was born on January 30, 1872, and died on January 17th, 1938, just 13 days before his 66th birthday and 7 years before I was born. His death certificate states that he died of bilateral sclerotic heart disease and hypostatic pneumonia. Hearsay has it that Grandpa Billy Leahy died on a cold day in January and the snow was knee deep to a tall Indian.

> **FORTY YEARS AGO**
> *in The Star*
>
> From Files of January 17, 1927
>
> Little Jack Little, popular singer, appeared this week as a guest artist on WDAF radio station.
>
> The Jackson County members in the Missouri House of Representatives now in session are William H. Lafferty, Max Asotsky, Richard Ray, N. R. Holcomb, M. H. Davis, John B. Haskell, Jerome Walsh, William Hicks, Clarence P. LeMire and William J. Leahy.
>
> Miss Georgia Hodges of Olathe, daughter of ex-Governor George H. Hodges, has been named editor-in-chief of the Legenda, publication of Wellesley college.
>
> A banking merger today gave the west business section of the Argentine district of Kansas City, Kansas, a financial institution with total deposits of $700,000. It was the consolidation of the Argentine State, Industrial State and the Mutual State banks into one to be known as the Industrial State bank.
>
> George Young, 17-year-old Canadian, yesterday swam the San Pedro channel off the California coast a distance of 22 miles, in 15 hours, 45 minutes, to take the $25,000 Catalina swim prize.
>
> R. V. Harman, head of the history department at Westport high school, goes to the University of Missouri next week on a leave of absence which breaks into 17½ years of continuous service as a Kansas City teacher.

I have been told that Billy Leahy and Mamie Foley met at a tavern owned by Keenan's on Cherry Street. They had three children. Margaret Elizabeth (Tootsie) was the oldest. My dad, William James (Bill) Leahy, Jr., was the middle child. Joseph (Joe) was the youngest. Politics were an integral part of their lives. Mamie was a respected confidant as the County Clerk/ Chief of Staff, to the Kansas City Mayor. My grandfather Leahy was a Missouri Legislator, the State Representative for the northeast part of Kansas City. Prior to him holding this office, John Leahy, his uncle, held the seat. Billy and Mamie initially lived at 9th and Garfield. Tom Pendergast, a political boss that controlled Kansas City at the time, wasn't happy when my grandparents moved to a home outside his district. Their new home was at 2927 Garfield. Pendergast fired Billy Leahy for moving outside his district.

I often heard the phrase, Pogue Malone, I think it means, Kiss My Arse. This was the environment in which my dad grew up.

Left, Mary Magdalene Foley Leahy, my paternal grandmother. Right, William James Leahy, my paternal grandfather.

Chapter 4

1960 to 1965

Martha: 15-20 Years of Age

As a Junior in high school, many of my friends had driver's licenses; and we spent our free time at Sidney's, Winstead's, or Allen's Drive-Ins, grabbing a burger and cherry limeade, or just sipping a coke. We could talk for hours, mostly about boys. I also met my first real boyfriend, Butch. A lot of people were shocked that I liked Butch. What was there not to like? He lettered in football at Rockhurst High School. He drove a great car. He was fun to be with. And, as it turns out, I am attracted to guys with a certain body type: football linemen.

My Junior year I was chosen by the Senior class to be a Prom Attendant along with Kathy Atchity. This was a big deal. Butch was my date. Shortly after prom, Butch and I broke up. I mean, he broke up with me. I often wondered if he stayed with me so he could escort the Prom Attendant. Well, no matter. I missed him.

I spent most Friday nights with my girlfriends. Jeanette Vail would usually drive and pick up three or four of us in the early evening. We might TP (toilet paper) a house or borrow a swan from Loose Park Lake. We frequently teepeed the Rockhurst College dorms. Once we almost got caught by one of the Rockhurst dorm guys but I hid under the eaves of a neighborhood house. I never considered the consequences. You could not do this today and should not have done it back then. We were lucky we didn't get hurt or worse.

Four years at STA made a big difference in my life. I had an excellent high school education. I had taken 4 years of Latin, one AP math course, and occasionally made the honor roll.

My first year of college was on the same campus as my high school. My mother was convinced that state universities were run by communists, and she didn't want me, or my siblings, to be exposed to harmful ideologies. Thus, I attended Avila College, a small liberal arts college for women, administered by the Sisters of St. Joseph of Carondelet. The dear Sisters educated me from kindergarten through my undergraduate college years. There was no question as to what my major would be. I enrolled in Nursing with a minor in Psychology. My mother understood poverty and never wanted her children to experience it. She often said, "As a nurse, you will always be able to get a job and support yourself if need be." I later read more into this message, i.e., just in case marriage doesn't work out you will be able to support yourself. "Besides," she said," it's good to have your own money."

By my sophomore year the college had moved five miles south where the campus was still under construction and only two of the proposed six buildings were habitable. At the time, window glazers were on strike, so there was no glass where there were window spaces. Mind you, Kansas City is cold and snowy in the winter, so it was not unusual to see students wearing gloves, hats, scarves, and coats in class. The good thing is that Avila College was a small local college, everyone knew each other, and the faculty were engaging and qualified.

I liked Philosophy, Anatomy-Physiology, and Logic. I started nursing clinicals in my junior year. Each semester, for the next two years, I gained experience working on medical-surgical units within St. Joseph's Hospital, in psychiatric hospitals, on pediatric units, and on gynecological and obstetrical units at Truman Medical Center (called General Hospital at the time). I liked psychiatric nursing but began to focus on patients with medical-surgical issues. I knew that working in the general field of nursing would be most helpful in reinforcing my education and preparing me for a specialty later in my career. I ran for Student Government President at Avila my senior year but lost to Edith Messina. I never thought much about the loss, but rather turned my attention and energy into founding the Avila Yearbook that was called Erica. I cannot remember where that name came from, but I do recall that we used a passage from the New Testament as our Yearbook theme. "For Everything there is a season, A time for every activity under heaven." Ecclesiastes 3:1-8.

During my junior year of college, I watched a 5-minute film produced by The March of Dimes that I still recall, "The Same Inside." The purpose of the film was to show that no matter what disability or illness one might have, no matter what we looked like, we are all the same inside, experiencing the same good, bad, happy, or sad emotions. A few years later, I would use the film as an assistant professor of nursing, to share with my students. It was important they understood that those they cared for were the same inside regardless of their disability, illness, color, race, or ethnicity.

I loved college. I got good grades. I had a great circle of friends. I learned to play bridge. I met my future husband on a blind date. I received scholastic and meritorious awards. However, it's interesting that no one explicitly told me back then that I had leadership qualities. I worked for years without realizing others saw me as a leader from a young age. Identifying one's strengths early on in life and telling another what you see in them is important. Words, both spoken and unspoken, have an effect.

Mary Helen, my older sister, married in 1962. Mother helped Mary Helen plan a beautiful wedding. She looked like a princess. I was her Maid of Honor. A morning wedding at Visitation Catholic Church, was followed by a formal champagne breakfast at Stephenson's Apple Orchard and then a reception with music and everyone dancing the polka. Mother and dad gave Mary Helen and her husband a down payment on a cute two-bedroom home in Westwood Hills, Kansas. Only later did we learn it had been a shotgun wedding.

From the early days of their marriage, things did not go well. Tom, my sister's husband, couldn't settle. In less than a year, Tom moved his family to Columbia, Missouri, where he started Medical School. Within a couple of years, he transferred to Ann Arbor, Michigan, to continue medical school, because it was a more prestigious university. His folly continued for years. He never graduated after years and years of financial support from my sister, who sometimes worked two jobs to support him and their five young children. This situation brought much sadness and conflict within our home as my sister started drinking to cope with her life situation. Mary Helen in many ways shared our family values. She was well educated. She was smart. She worked hard, and she loved and cared for her five children. However, the stress and responsibility led to self-destructive behavior. Her husband had none of these redeeming values. Later, he would be arrested and sent to jail.

My dad loved sports and was a true University of Missouri fan, a tiger through and through. He loved to stay up at night (by himself) and listen to the local baseball games on the radio. He sat at the kitchen table with his head down on the tabletop occasionally smoking and rooting for the Kansas City A's. Dad liked to bowl, and he loved watching Jackie Gleeson and the Honeymooners and Bob Hope on TV. He always called me when Martha Ray was on TV. He thought she was so funny. That's when I began to hate my name. I thought Martha Ray had such a big loudmouth (literally and figuratively) and I didn't want to be anything like her. Why had they named me Martha? Of course, my older sister was Mary, and my younger sister was Elizabeth. I had to be Martha, the one in the Bible that Jesus had to remind what was important in life.

Dad had bad teeth. He admitted that he seldom saw a dentist growing up. The day he had all his teeth pulled I remember him sitting in the living room in his rocking chair and watching him apply ice packs to his jaws. It must have really hurt to have all his teeth pulled, even if many of them were decayed. His gums were swollen. It was days before he could fit his new dentures. Dad sat in the same rocking chair after his mother died. He was lost in deep thought for days. It was quiet around home then.

Dad loved stewed tomatoes, fried chicken and fried liver. He loved sweets even more. It's sad to recall that dad ate alone most nights. Mother was always anxious to get dinner over with so she and us kids ate between 5:00 and 6:00 pm. Many nights Dad didn't get home till after 6:30 pm, and

Mom would heat up his dinner, and he would eat alone at the table in the kitchen. There were few opportunities for us to talk as a family as I got older.

Dad began stopping at a local bar before coming home in the evening, always having a shot of whiskey followed by a beer. This habit became more frequent as he got older. While my childhood resonates with the sounds of kick the can, tag, hide and seek, and red rover, red rover, my teenage years resonate with whispers and tears from embarrassment. My father began to drink more as I and my siblings got older. Dad always drank but not to excess. I am not sure why it increased. I know there is a genetic component to it, but I imagine being in an unhappy marriage, supporting five children that were all getting older, my mother's depression after her mother's death, and the mounting stresses at work affected his drinking pattern. It wasn't just the drinking that was bad, it was the arguments that led to Dad walking out of our home, saying he wouldn't be back.

Alcoholism would have a long-lasting impact on me and my siblings. However, sometimes good things come from hard times. The sadness and humiliation from seeing my father stewed and barely able to walk up the hill to our home in the evenings pushed me forward in life. Consciously, I wanted to distinguish myself from this behavior, this sadness, this illness, and the arguing within our home. I seldom talked about my family in public, yet I knew others talked about my family in private. I became the peacemaker in the family. Unfortunately, I would always have trouble confronting family issues. Wearing a smile and working hard were easier. Those traits began to define me.

Dad never missed a day of work before his 52nd birthday. That's when he had his first heart attack. The doctors didn't think he would make it. My mother and I spent almost three days at the hospital waiting around the clock for some updates on his health. Gradually he got better and was able to come home and eventually go back to work. I was hoping that if Dad was well enough to come home, the relationship between him and my mother might improve. My mom and dad were very different people. I can see that now, years later. They had many of the same values, including family, education, and faith. They both worked hard – just in different ways. Both were strongly influenced by their parents. Mother, controlled by her mother, became more rigid and demanding in her expectations of others. She feared poverty as her parents had. Dad worked hard but also played hard.

On my 18th birthday, my parents gave me a pearl ring, and Dad continued his tradition and gave me a silver dollar, as well. President Dwight D. Eisenhower's face is on most of the silver dollars I've collected over the years.

I was diagnosed with a duodenal ulcer at age 19. My coping mechanisms worked on the outside, but it didn't protect me from what was happening inside my body. I smoked occasionally on campus to be part of the crowd. I improved my bridge game. I loved being defined as cerebral. However, not being more active and athletic has hurt me. Scared and embarrassed by the dysfunction in my family, I was always hiding what was going on in the family, but I was also always smiling.

On December 5th, 1964, I agreed to a blind date with a fraternity guy who was coming into town from the University of Kansas. This was an annual trip for a group of fraternity brothers. The guys never knew anything about the girl they were being fixed up with, rather they were just looking for a fun time in Kansas City prior to the holiday break. I wasn't concerned about my date; I had already seen his picture and thought he was cute. Plus, I trusted my friend, Betty Wolf, to fix me up with a nice guy. I stayed upstairs in my bedroom until my date arrived. I wore a new pair of green silk nubby ankle length pants with a tailored white long sleeve blouse that tied at the neck. As I descended the stairs, I immediately noticed my date was in a navy-blue suit with a striped, blue tie. He looked older and very much the fraternity guy. He was also wearing a cute smile.

There were five college guys that night that were fixed up with my friends. It was a fun evening. I got home before one in the morning as was the rule and didn't think much more about my blind date. Three weeks later, I got a postcard from him and realized he had kept my name and my address. He wanted to see me again. That spring, Rodd David Staker and I began dating. He introduced me to university life and Sigma Phi Epsilon fraternity parties. On many weekends I traveled to Lawrence, Kansas, and stayed in the Chi Omega sorority house with friends so we could attend parties or dances on Saturday nights.

Rodd David Staker, 21 years of age.

Rodd was a junior in college and in the Navy ROTC (Reserved Officer Training Corp) program. He headed to California for his summer cruise in June of 1965. He loves to tell people it was the first time he had seen the ocean. However, the Navy came natural to him as his dad had been a Navy Pilot during World War II and was not only awarded the Purple Heart but also the Silver Star for his bravery and courage helping crew members on the USS Wasp survive a direct hit from a Japanese suicide bomber.

ΣΦE *Bowery Brawl*
November 5, 1965

Major influencers and the lessons I was learning at this stage of my life:

During this critical developmental age, I was beginning to understand more about myself and who I wanted to be. These are the critical memories I most often recall.

- It was 1960, when I first became interested in what was happening politically in the country. I had watched the presidential debate between John Fitzgerald Kennedy and Richard Nixon on TV and thought Kennedy was a great candidate for presidency. I even shook his hand when he was in an open car parade through downtown Kansas City, Missouri. Everyone at STA knew I was politically aware at the time, and I talked openly about Kennedy as the next President of the United States. Prior to the presidential election in the Fall of 1960, I was called into the principal's office at Saint Teresa's Academy (STA) and told I had been selected by the faculty to participate in the all-school presidential debate. Sister Anna Joseph, CSJ, asked if I accept this challenge? This was quite an honor since I was a first semester Junior. I and another student would debate the two candidates running for the Presidency of the United States of America in front of the whole student body. I was so excited. I immediately said, "Yes, I will do it." As I was already thinking about the debate and my strategies the principal said there was only one stipulation. "Martha, you will represent and debate on behalf of the Republican nominee, Richard Nixon." With hesitation and apprehension, I accepted the challenge. This is one of the most helpful experiences of my life. I was forced to look at both sides of the coin. I got a Nixon straw hat and large Nixon Republican Pin for my jacket. I came to the debate armed with knowledge. I addressed John F. Kennedy's weaknesses but more importantly emphasized Richard Nixon's strengths. Some say I won the debate.

I learned that it is important to listen and not talk until the other person has finished speaking. You may not know what you agree to if you don't listen. I also learned that it is important to **understand both sides of an issue** if you are going to be an effective debater and if you want to be a change agent.

- Dr. Steve Sirridge, Professor of Psychology at Avila University, said during a regular class period, "Ask for what you want. Others may not know what you want or need." I immediately raised my hand. I asked, "You mean if I have to ask someone to tell me they love me it doesn't diminish their true feelings". Dr. Sirridge replied, "No, another person may not know what you need. Others cannot read your mind. Don't forget that person still has a choice. They can either tell you, give you, or help you get what you need or NOT." I thought others should know what I needed. I thought I needed to do everything, be everything. I thought I had something to prove. I didn't ask for help because I thought it reflected weakness.

I learned to **"ask for what you want"**. Most people feel more comfortable around someone who asks for help occasionally. **No one is perfect**.

- I did not attend my brother, Michael's, graduation from Rockhurst High School. No one in our family went to his graduation. There had been an argument and Michael left home and walked 3 miles in his tuxedo to his graduation, alone. Part of this was my fault. My mom asked me to stay home that evening and care for my younger sister. I said no that I had other plans. I don't know where my dad was or any of my other siblings. I just know that my mother couldn't get anyone to stay with my sister so she decided she wouldn't go. I wish I could do this over. I would stay home and there could be a different outcome. Even now, 50 years later, I am sad as I look back on my brother's milestone. Such a painful memory.

I learned it is important to **be there for your child or your family**. Sometimes you must put others before yourself. It is important to tell your child they did a good job, and you are proud of them. I am truly sorry, Michael. My brother's graduation was so much more important than anything I was going to do.

I was also learning at this time:

Don't say things you don't mean; you cannot take them back. People never forget what another says to them, especially when it emotionally hurts.

If you don't succeed at one thing, **try** another.

The Reader's most significant memories and influences from fifteen to twenty years of age:

Chapter 5

1965 to 1970

Martha: 20-25 Years of Age

It is hard to comprehend what happened over the next five years. I moved to Colorado, earned a graduate degree in nursing, got engaged, married, had a baby, and taught part-time at Avila College/University.

Flash back. Spring semester, 1966, I became a Sigma Phi Epsilon Sweetheart. The traditional ceremonial presentation of Rodd giving me his Sig Ep fraternity pin, as the entire fraternity in dress blue sport coats sang the *Sigma Phi Epsilon Sweetheart* song, intimated that Rodd and I might someday become engaged. Back then college students would say I was engaged to be engaged - it sounds silly now. I loved Rodd but when he talked about marriage, I wasn't ready. Rodd would be fulfilling his three-year commitment in the U.S. Navy immediately upon college graduation and would most likely be assigned to a ship heading to the Western Pacific Ocean. We decided to wait and see what happened. Parked on an old farm road in Lawrence, Kansas, we each promised to carry within us the memories we had made together and the future dreams we envisioned.

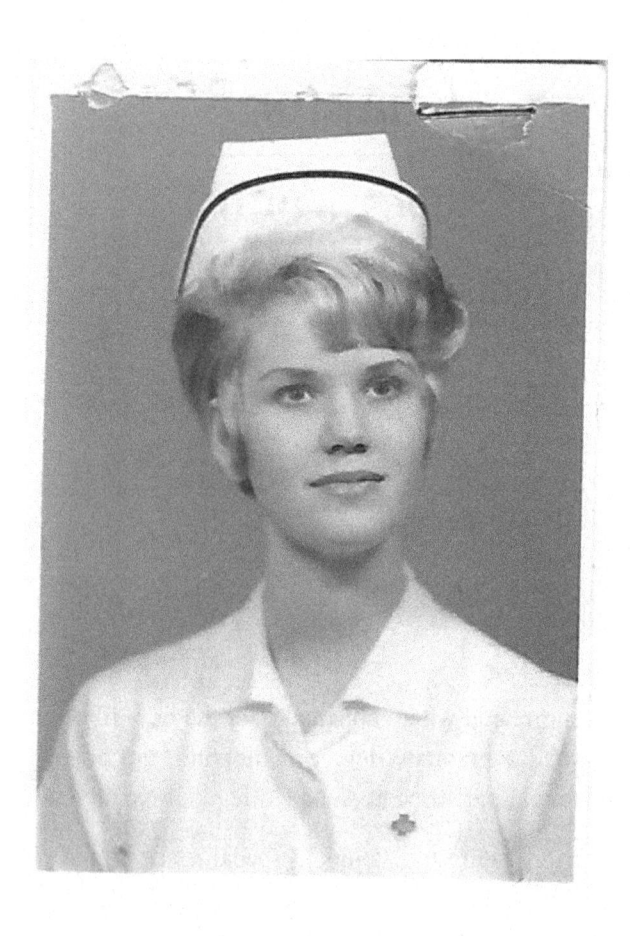

In 1966, I graduated from Avila College with a Bachelor of Science degree in Nursing. My first job was at Baptist Memorial Hospital, 3rd floor, helping care for 56 patients on the medical-surgical unit. My initial salary was $5,200 a year. As soon as the Personnel Office at the Hospital was notified that I had successfully passed my Missouri State Boards in Nursing and was a Registered Nurse in the State of Missouri, I was put on the night shift (11 pm to 7 am) with only a Licensed Practical Nurse (LPN) to help me. It was horrible. The stress of being a new nurse without a mentor or support system was overwhelming. Within six months on the job, I was diagnosed with thyroiditis - an autoimmune illness- and had to take some time off. After several months of rest, I applied for a job at St. Joseph Hospital, the old Saint Joseph Hospital located at 2500 East Linwood, Kansas City, Missouri. The head nurse on 3 West was terrific, and it was there that I gained practical experience and confidence in my ability to care for hospitalized patients. I became the nurse everyone called when they needed help starting an IV or placing a nasogastric tube. Back then nurses still wore white uniforms, nursing pins reflecting the program from which they graduated, and white nursing caps. Nursing caps with a black stripe across the front meant you were a registered nurse. Nursing caps without the black stripe meant you were a student studying to be a nurse.

Within days of my graduation, Rodd graduated from the University of Kansas with a Bachelor of Science degree in Civil Engineering. Rodd had impressed me with his slide rule and pocket protector. He was not only fun but smart and caring. The day he graduated he was commissioned as an officer in the US Navy and assigned to the USS Merrick AKA 97. Ensign Staker had to report for duty in days and would be heading to Vietnam in the fall. The United Stakes had become heavily engaged militarily in the Vietnam War in the early 1960's. Anti-war and peace demonstrations occurred throughout the United States, particularly on university campuses. Some men left the United States to live in Canada to avoid the draft.

I visited Rodd in Long Beach, California, before he shipped out to Vietnam. We had a wonderful time. I had no idea how dangerous his next three years of service would be. After two years on the USS Merrick 97, an attack cargo ship operating in the South China Sea and Vietnam, Rodd was transferred to the USS Iwo Jima, that carried 1000 marines and their helicopters, headed to Vietnam. As officer of the deck underway, he made decisions that affected the lives of many.

I can so clearly remember the first Christmas Rodd was away. A large box arrived for me in the mail postmarked from the Philippines. Inside was a handmade wooden jewelry chest with antique gold hardware. The chest had 6 drawers, each held shut with tape for travel even though a key assured the contents were secure. As I opened each drawer, I found a special and meaningful gift inside. There was a beautiful seashell from the beach, there were notes that expressed Rodd's love. I cherish this gift now more than ever.

After Rodd left for the Navy, a colleague told me "Distance makes the heart grow fonder," and then added "for someone else." But that's not what happened. For three years, letters and gifts made their way back and forth between us. There were 3:00 am phone calls if a phone line became available when the ship was in port, there were orchids from Hawaii, and there were brief visits, in either Denver or California, between his tours of duty in Vietnam. I remember Rodd visiting me in Denver on Thanksgiving, 1968. I baked a turkey and all the fixings for the first time. It was then we both knew we wanted to spend the rest of our lives together.

In 1968, I was accepted into the University of Colorado's School of Nursing graduate program and began work toward a Master of Science Degree in Nursing. I have my older sister, Mary Helen, to thank for encouraging me to attend graduate school. Mary Helen, who was a registered nurse, encouraged me to apply for a government grant to advance my nursing education and credentials. In the late 60's there were very few baccalaureate prepared nurses, and even fewer nurses with a master's degree. The need for more nurses led the federal government to offer baccalaureate prepared nurses grants to complete a Master of Science degree in Nursing. The grant would cover tuition and books and provide a monthly stipend of $250.00 to help with living expenses. The grant had only one condition, I had to agree to stay active and contribute to the profession of nursing, advancing, and supporting its growth throughout my life.

At the time, there were five universities that offered federal grants to nurses wishing to receive a master's degree in nursing. After working for almost two years as a staff nurse on medical-surgical units, I applied to the closest school, the University of Colorado Graduate School of Nursing, and was accepted. I moved to Denver and rented an apartment at 816 Cherry near the University of Colorado Medical Center.

I chose a graduate track of studies which emphasized Teaching, Curriculum Development, and Research. Socially, I bloomed. Carol Campagna (aka, CC) from Buffalo New York, and Dorothy Batton (aka,

DB) from Houston, Texas became lifelong friends and shared this amazing experience with me. It was the first time I was truly on my own, with my own apartment and my own car. I had purchased a new 1968 red Volkswagen beetle, with manual transmission, prior to moving to Colorado. Together with CC and DB I attended Cheyenne Days in Wyoming, skied in Breckenridge, visited the pub in Georgetown, attended concerts at Red Rocks and found time to study. Going away – getting away from my family - was good. Rodd was in Vietnam, and this was an opportunity for me to grow and become more independent.

Judy Kiernan and Sue Huether were two of the faculty that oversaw the syllabus of one of my graduate courses at the University of Colorado School of Nursing. Many of us in the class didn't think the core content of the course met our educational needs. So, the faculty allowed the enrolled graduate students to re-design the course syllabus. It was a great learning opportunity for me. My friends, CC and DB, and I worked to design and publish a new syllabus. Graduate school became a maturing process and it gave me the credentials necessary to move forward with my career.

At the end of my second semester at CU, I flew home to Kansas City for the Christmas break. On Christmas night, 1968, Rodd proposed. I accepted. The timing was right.

Lt. JG, Rodd David Staker honorably departed the Navy in May 1969, at the end of his three-year commitment and I graduated from the University of Colorado with a Master of Science degree in Nursing one week later. I was ready to marry the wonderful man I met on a blind date five years earlier. The summer of 69 was fun as we both had time to plan a September wedding. My mother took me shopping not only for a wedding dress but also for a complete trousseau. We found just the right wedding gown and veil at Swanson's Department Store on the Country Club Plaza. Then Mother and I went downtown where she bought me a "going away" two-piece red suit, a brown and white check dress, a summer short navy and white polka dot dress, and a three-piece red and yellow plaid suit that included a skirt, blouse, and matching vest. I had a lingerie shower. I was set. My mother was very sweet and helped me. What a great memory I have of this with my mother.

September 6, 1969

The day we got married was bright and sunny, not a cloud in the deep blue sky. Monsignor Arthur M. Tighe married us at Visitation Catholic church and our reception was held at the Plaza III on the Country Club Plaza. I will never forget how happy I was that day.

We honeymooned for two weeks. We spent one week in San Francisco staying at the St. Francis Hotel and another week on Mission Beach, California, where Rodd sprained his ankle on the beach the first night we were there. What can I say? He was the butt of many jokes related to how he got crutches. While flying home to Kansas City, Rodd revealed that we would have season tickets to all the KU football and basketball games for the rest of our lives. I had not heard this before we married and had no idea the impact KU would have on our life in the coming decades.

We returned home, and I began a new job as a clinical instructor of Medical-Surgical Nursing at Avila University. Within a couple of months, I realized I was pregnant. Nine months and 5 days from the day we married, I delivered our first healthy baby boy, David Matthew Staker, 6 pounds, 2 ounces and 20 inches long. Although the labor was only three hours, the pain was intense. When Rodd held my hand, the pain seemed to lessen. I will never forget what his touch meant that night. We were in this together, and he carried half the pain.

The day after David was born, the nurses who were caring for me saw Rodd come into my hospital room. They were laughing and talking between themselves. Then one of the nurses asked me if that was my husband. When I said yes, they said they were afraid the night before that Rodd wouldn't make it as they watched him pace the floor. They had never seen a more nervous expectant father. Back then fathers were not allowed in the delivery suite. What a shame. I might not have needed any anesthesia if he had been there holding my hand.

Although I continued to teach part-time after David was born, I decided to take a break the following year as we were expecting our second child.

If you are familiar with the Holmes-Rahe Life Stress Inventory: The Social Readjustment Rating Scale, you will understand that this was not just a fun year but a stressful time. The Holmes-Rahe scale is used to gauge the impact of changes and stress in one's life. My score was high.

Major influencers and lessons I was learning at this stage of my life:

Every day I was learning something new. Most importantly, I began to realize I wasn't always right, and everybody didn't think like me. The three life experiences that I readily recall and continue to inform my life are described below.

- I was a brand-new graduate nurse. A patient I was caring for at Baptist Memorial Hospital died. The death was expected. Since I had never cared for a patient after death, the Head Nurse told me how to care for the body and then how to transport the body to the morgue on the lower level of the hospital. After the body was placed on the gurney, I was to cover the patient's body with a sheet and take the body down the front set of employee elevators to the lowest level of the hospital, level B. Prior to pushing the body down the long hallway, I was to close each patient's door to make sure they didn't see me. I listened carefully but thought I had a better idea. I would take the body down the back elevator closer to the patient's room. I knew the elevator went to the "B" level of the hospital. So, I pushed the gurney onto the back elevator and pushed the "B" button. As the elevator doors opened, I pushed the gurney out. I was in the middle of the kitchen! The cooks and dietary staff were stunned. I quickly pulled the gurney back onto the elevator, hit the button back to "3", and quietly and cautiously pushed the body down the long hallway to the front set of employee elevators and to the morgue. No one on the 3rd floor knew what I had done. Everyone in the kitchen knew what I had done.

I learned it is important to **listen carefully and follow directions**. Others may know what is best.

- Kathryn Smith was a professor at the University of Colorado's Graduate School of Nursing. She was older than the other faculty and I took what she had to say for granted. I thought her class would be a breeze. Looking back, Dr. Smith was ahead of her time. The major assignment in her class was to develop a handbook that forced the nurse to make health care decisions about patients they were caring for. Once a decision was made the reader would turn to the page that described the outcome that resulted from the chosen choice or decision. If you didn't like the outcome you had to move forward and make better decisions in the future. It was a difficult assignment and required time, research, and creativity. This approach is frequently used as a teaching tool today, but it was innovative in the 60's and difficult without the support of a computer. Well, I put off the assignment thinking I would do it over the Christmas break, but when I got engaged, I was too excited to work on it. I pulled something together at the last minute. I disappointed myself and regret that I didn't turn in a better product to such a deserving professor. I felt I disrespected Professor Smith.

Professor Smith also did something no other professor of mine had ever done. She took our class to the Boulder Country Club for lunch prior to the Christmas Holiday. She had pre-ordered our lunch and selected foods I had not tasted. I specifically remember the Avocado-Grapefruit salad with French dressing. It was delicious. Dr. Smith was a very caring, smart woman who I remember with great respect.

I learned to **Respect one's age and the wisdom and foresight they have. I learned not to disappoint myself let alone my professor.**

- As part of a research project in graduate school I volunteered in the cardiology lab where I assisted with cardioversions. One day during a cardioversion procedure, the patient was already asleep, the cardiologist asked me where I had been "trained". I quickly replied, "I was not trained, I was educated." Luckily, I didn't add "like a cat or dog". The room went quiet, and no one spoke. Over and over during my undergraduate education, nursing faculty had emphasized that as baccalaureate prepared nurses we had been educated and not trained. This was to differentiate baccalaureate prepared nurses from 3-year hospital "trained" nurses. My remarks to the cardiologist were a regurgitation of what I had heard for years. Immediately following the procedure, the physician told me to get out of his lab and never come back. Later in the year we saw each other in the University's Library and spoke. I'd like to think we both learned something. Also, it is important to note the patient did well.

I learned to **think before you speak and learn from one's mistakes**.

I was also learning at this time:

If you are going to **respect yourself**, you must **do the right thing.**

Family means helping each other reach their goals. My sister, Mary Helen, had helped me get a graduate degree.

The Readers' most significant memories and influencers from twenty to twenty-five years of age:

Chapter 6

1970 to 1975

Martha: 25 to 30 Years of Age

Living on the second floor of an apartment building with no elevator and two babies isn't easy. Daniel Christopher was born 22 months after David on April 14th, 1972, weighing 8lbs, 15 ounces, and 22 inches long. He weighed nearly 3 lbs. more than his older brother at birth.

Daniel Christopher was a beautiful baby.

To use a washer and dryer, Rodd and I had to go outside and enter the laundry room through a basement door. However, the apartment was affordable and located in an area convenient to Rodd's work and our families. It had two bedrooms, a dining room, front room, kitchen and one bathroom. When the current managers of the apartment building moved, Rodd and I applied to become apartment managers. The owners hired us immediately. I was responsible for renting the apartments. Rodd was responsible for cleaning/vacuuming the halls and stairways, cleaning the apartments when tenants moved out and chlorinating and managing the swimming pool. It was a lot for Rodd, since he worked 40 to 50 hours a week as a consulting civil engineer. However, this arrangement allowed us to live in the apartment complex rent free for two years and save $180 a month to make a down payment on a home.

By October of 1972, we decided we had to move. Danny was 6 months old and had colic. He often cried at night. There was no place for the boys to play outside. My patience had run out. It was hard staying home every day in an apartment with an infant and toddler. One Sunday, we headed out in our 1968 red Volkswagen beetle to find a house. Having grown up in Kansas City, I thought we should look in the Brookside neighborhood. There was a For Sale sign on a two-story home on 70th street that looked nice. Beautiful elm trees in their fall colors lined 70th street. We walked through the house quickly and decided within 48 hours to buy it. We never even looked at another house or property. We were so tired and worn out that all we wanted was a home of our own. We initially liked the dark green shag carpet throughout the first floor of the home. We thought we could tolerate the thick sprayed bumpy plastered ceilings. However, the portable dishwasher was an issue. It had to be moved from the east wall to the west wall of the kitchen and connected to the kitchen sink spout each time it was used. That meant we could only enter the kitchen by bending down below the dishwasher hoses when it was running and getting water from the kitchen faucets had to be postponed for two hours. We considered the water heated radiators a blessing while we were sure that a single large window air conditioner and attic fan would cool the two-story home on hot summer days.

We convinced ourselves that the house had the bones of what we would need in the future. I remember saying, "We could live here forever." It was an older English Tudor home built by J.C. Nichols. In fact, we found literature that said our future home was the showcase home of J. C. Nichols in 1928. There were 4 bedrooms, a side room for an office, a fireplace, and a large kitchen with an attached screen porch. We were blind to the fact that the entire house, 44 years old, needed to be updated. We signed the papers for the house on Friday, November 13th, 1972. It was one of the luckiest days of our life. We moved in the next day. We had found the perfect neighborhood. With more than 80 children on the block, there was going to be a village to support family life. Little did we know that it would take the next 50 years to get each room in the house updated. Life was happening, and the house could wait. We were raising our children, building lifelong friendships, and working. Fifty years later, it has absolutely become the home we could stay in for the rest of our lives.

On May 24th, 1971, my grandpa, the Mick, died. He was one month short of 89 years of age; I was 26. He was my last living grandparent. Grandpa had seen it all, from horse and buggies, the first cars, first flights, and the first man on the moon.

My father died the next year on June 21st, 1972. Dad was only 59. My mother was 57 years of age, and I was 27. Dad liked the man I married even though he was a KU Jayhawk. Before his death, Dad was able to hold David, then 2 years of age and Danny then 2 months old. Dad knew that I was happy, and he was happy for me. I had not been close to my father. In our family you had to pick sides. I found myself on my mother's side. Years later, I would have a more objective view of our family and realize my dad never missed a paycheck in supporting us and he loved each of us. Family dynamics or family systems have a tremendous impact on children growing up and their future. With age comes perspective. With age and time, the good memories flood back clouding much of the hurt and sadness. However, one never forgets the bad times. We only dilute them with new experiences, new memories. (See Appendix D for additional information on my father's family.)

On October 14th, 1973, our baby girl was born, weighing 7lbs ten ounces at 7:10 pm. Rodd wanted to name our beautiful baby Suzie, and I wanted to name her Bridget. We settled on Bridget Suzanne. Once again, I was on my own throughout labor since fathers were still not allowed in the delivery room. We were so happy to welcome a little girl into our family. There had not been any girls born into the Staker family for decades. It was a time of celebration. I was also elated as disposable diapers were just coming into stores and I could say goodbye to the pink van pulling up in front of our home delivering clean diapers semi-weekly and the fragrance of ammonia that permeated the nursery.

That December Rodd and I began a tradition that lasted 24 years. The Sunday night before Christmas, Mr. and Mrs. Claus visited our home. Santa and Mrs. Claus told stories about stinky cheese, stinky feet, and socks under the bed. Santa and Mrs. Claus never left the glow of our fireplace until they held each child, no matter what their age. Imagine seeing a 21-year-old on Santa's lap, grinning, and telling Santa that they had been good and what they wanted for Christmas. It was a magical night! Our closest friends and their children shared this special night with us over the years. After Santa and Mrs. Claus flew off to visit other children, we enjoyed the traditional dinner of ham and egg rolls, Swiss cheese, cranberry salad, and McLain's chocolate thumb-print cookies.

David talks with Mrs. Claus.

Bridget and Danny listen to Mrs. Claus' stories.

Rodd shares his Christmas list with Santa. Has he been good this year?

While Rodd was working long days as a design engineer and resident engineer on several construction projects, I was managing at home and serving lunch most days to six or seven children. Small tables and chairs on the screen porch made cleaning up easier. A rotating menu of hot dogs and Kool Aid, mac and cheese, or peanut butter and jelly sandwiches satisfied even the hungriest child. Our dog, Dolly, half schnauzer and half dachshund, made swift work of the crumbs and leftovers.

My staying home and not working left us with little discretionary money, so we made a conscious decision to spend our money on what was most important to us, our children's early education. All three of the children attended Ward Parkway preschool for two years and then went to Saint Elizabeth Catholic grade school. When I asked our children, later as adults, if they wish they had gone to a different grade school, one that might have offered them a foreign language and a greater emphasis on STEM (science, technology, engineering, and math) studies or the arts, they answered in unison, "No, Saint Elizabeth's is where we got our values and made lifelong friends."

My St. Teresa's Academy high school friends kept me sane during this time. We were all pretty much in the same boat back then and could complain to each other about pregnancy, labor and delivery, motherhood, and whatever else was bothering us at the time. We babysat each other's children and shared easy to make recipes. We observed each other's child rearing practices with approval or disbelief. We learned how to clean and organize our homes or not. We played bridge together while our children played in the adjoining room. No matter, we accepted each other and remained friends through all of it.

Sitting (L to R): Sharon Everett, JoAnn Rushing, Kathy Frey. Standing (L to R): Aileen Richmond, Judy DiBella, Martha, Cathy Marx, and Betsy Rushton.

In the fall of 1974, Rodd decided to use the G I Bill and return to school. He planned to earn an MBA (Master of Business Administration). It was a major decision because he would continue to work full-time and attend classes in the evening. Weekends would include study time and time to complete assignments. It would take 5 years for him to receive his MBA with an emphasis on Finance, since he did not have an undergraduate degree in business. I agreed with this plan, but I must admit at times it was hard. There were a lot of dinners, bath times, and weekends he wasn't home, when I needed his help. However, as the old saying goes, "No pain, no gain." Later his MBA would serve us well, and I would be the one to go back to school to earn a second master's degree, and he would encourage and support me.

I had kept secrets from my husband when we dated and during the early years of our marriage.

The Irish have often hidden things from their past and present, and I was part of this, hiding and burying secrets deep within me. Then one day, I started crying and it all came out. My Dad was an alcoholic. I had been afraid to share the turmoil and embarrassment I experienced growing up. I was afraid to tell him the impact this had had not only on me but the whole family. I worried he'd regret marrying me. However, when so much happens around you that you can't hide it any longer the truth has to come out. I miscalculated love. Rodd only loved me more.

Major influencers and lessons I was learning at this stage of my life:

With such major life experiences occurring during this period of my life, I most often recall three memories that would seem negligible to another person. Yet, these have been critical to my overall mental health and happiness.

- We were still living in the apartment on the Plaza. We purchased a fish tank with several goldfish. One afternoon, I noticed David putting his hand inside the fishbowl, trying to catch a goldfish. I yelled at David, "Don't do that you are acting like a two-year-old." He was a two-year-old. What was I thinking?

I learned it is important to understand **developmental stages and readiness**. Expect from another only what that person can do. I knew this from my textbooks and now I understood it in real life.

- I remember sitting on our gold striped velvet sofa and telling Rodd about my family and the history of alcoholism and the embarrassment I had felt growing up. I remember Rodd telling me it was okay. It didn't change him or his feelings for me and my family. He still enjoyed my dad and my mom.

I learned **secrets are harmful to one's health and emotional life. Being truthful and transparent feels better.** I was emotionally much healthier.

- I wanted to be perfect. I needed to show strength. I couldn't ask for help. I remember rushing one day to get to a friend's home to play cards even though I wasn't feeling well. I needed my friends and others to see me as a person who could manage and keep it all together. It was a hard time for me.

It is important to **Love yourself and set priorities**. Believe in your **self-worth.**

I was also learning at this time:

Work hard and save your money.

It is important to have a support group and **build one's social capital.**

Healthy relationships are reciprocal.

The Reader's most significant memories and influences from twenty-five to thirty years of age:

Chapter 7

1975 to 1980

Martha: 30-35 Years of Age

EVERYDAY SEEMED MUCH like the other. Get up, make breakfast, dress the children, change diapers, clean the house, do laundry, and make dinner. I would try to take a nap some afternoons, but it was hard with three preschoolers. I invested in books, and as David got older, he took to reading "The Hardy Boys" during nap time while Danny loved Beverly Cleary books, like "Ramona the Pest" and "Henry and the Paper Route." Bridget played with her Barbie dolls. I occasionally fell off to sleep only to wake up minutes later, fearful that the children were missing or hurt. I looked forward to the biweekly bridge with my girlfriends. I also looked forward to a date with Rodd, although date nights were rare in our first few years of marriage.

One's lifestyle has its consequences. At age 30, I wasn't feeling well. I was tired all the time. One doctor suggested that I was suffering from "cabin fever" and I just needed my husband to take me out more often or on a vacation. However, this didn't explain why I was having frequent episodes of pre-ventricular contractions (PVC's) and on occasion a heart rate of 160 per minute. A cardiologist diagnosed me with hyper-beta-adrenergic syndrome: too much adrenalin at times. I needed to limit my coffee intake, exercise more, and take Inderal, a beta blocker medication. I got better, but it took some time. Rodd had completed his MBA in 1979, so this helped. And my mother took all three children swimming several afternoons a week that summer, so I could nap. Our children loved their grandma taking them to Oceans of Fun and to the health club pool at 51st and Main.

I was 32 years of age and had not worked (let me make this clear -outside the home) for the last 6 years. I got a call from Sister Barbara Moore, CSJ, asking me to come teach with her. Avila's School of Nursing was now offering registered nurses that had graduated with an Associate of Arts degree or a three-year hospital diploma, a way to advance their academic credentials and earn a Bachelor of Science degree in Nursing. It would be a part-time job teaching 3 days a week. I wanted to go back to work, but my concern in saying yes was the children: Bridget was only 3 ½, Danny 5, and David 7. I would need to find the right person to care for them in my absence and I would need to arrange carpools so that I could participate in the driving but not on the days I worked. I did not want to compromise our children's early education.

I ran an ad in the Saint Elizabeth's Church bulletin as I thought that would be a good place to find a woman who would be caring and loving to the children. Joanna Unser answered the ad. When I first met her, I guessed she was about 70 years old. She was a soft-spoken woman with thick grey, wiry, natural curly hair. Her husband had died years earlier. She was short, stocky, slow to move, and walked with a slight limp. Her references were good. After spending time with her, I was convinced she was the perfect person to care for our children. She had never had children of her own and "loved on" the children she cared for according to her references. The arrangements were made. I would pick Joanna up and bring her to our home three mornings a week. Since our three children were attending different schools, having her in our home worked best. She would always be there to see the children picked up in the morning and would be there when they got home. Joanna Unser cared for our children for two years. She got to know all the neighborhood children and knew which ones she needed to watch more carefully. Each morning when I picked her up at her Troost apartment, she had a box of Nabisco lemon cooler cookies hidden under her coat or in her purse even though I had asked her not to bring them. Only later did I find out that Joanna was 78 years old when she started caring for our children. Our children were blessed to have her in their lives. She loved them. Danny would tell me it was okay for me to go to work when he was sick because Joanna was coming.

I began teaching at Avila University and would do so for the next six years, 1977 to 1983. I loved teaching. There was an old saying at Avila, part-time is full-time and full-time is all the time. I didn't save any money that first year of teaching; all the money went into childcare. But that was ok. I was healthier and loved the intellectual stimulation and social interactions. I was part of a team that taught and supported nurses that wanted to advance their education and earn a Bachelor of Science degree in Nursing. It was an ideal job. I worked part-time; I could flex some of my hours; and I was able to focus on concepts and leadership skills rather than more basic instructional course content. The students were older and more interested in learning. They had all been practicing nurses and understood the importance of interdisciplinary systems of care and the psychosocial aspects of wellness.

My love of teaching started early in my life when I was given a chance to help younger campers and students. In high school, I realized that I liked speaking and writing. I liked being creative, combining unrelated images or ideas to make course content new and more interesting. I think Sister Damien's English class my sophomore year in high school had a lot to do with this. Sister had us read *Catcher in the Rye*. She had us write poetry. She had us write an essay whereby we gave an inanimate object life. She pushed us to think creatively and make something great from what others saw as ordinary. I will never forget Concetta, my classmate, giving life to a cigarette butt that was discarded out of a car window and floated into the sewer system. What a life that cigarette butt lived, according to Concetta.

No matter the subject matter in school or while I was teaching, I began written and oral assignments by conceiving a way to make the subject matter more relatable and fun. I often used self-disclosure to help others identify with me or props like a board game to get students' attention. When I was teaching at an all-girl's private college (Avila University), I showed up once in a mini skirt, sat on the desk, spread my legs and chewed bubble gum as I discussed the characteristics of an effective leader. The images, content, and feedback are memorable. Approval from peers and colleagues inspired me to work even harder at being creative. At night I would often lie awake in bed writing my next paper or preparing for my next oral presentation. I was always working to find a way to engage others. As a part of my graduate school requirements at the University of Missouri-Kansas City, I completed a year's practicum, working with the chronically and terminally ill, at Research Medical Center. While I was there the health care team was worried about a young man who was dying of cancer. He had not talked with any staff and seemed withdrawn and sad. The health care team asked me to talk with him. Once I found out he was an engineer I knew what I would tell him. "I'm married to an engineer." That said it all. The connection was made.

Christmas Day of 1977, our family and extended family were sitting at our dining room table. It was about 6 pm. We had just finished devouring turkey, dressing, and all the usual sides, when we heard a loud noise over the fireplace in the living room. A large glass mirror, 60" by 40", that hung over the fireplace mantel, was cracking. Rodd and I ran into the living room, he warned me not to touch the mirror. It was red hot. The east wall of our living room was on fire. I called 911. Rodd and his brother took the children outside and placed them safely in a van. I began carrying out our new living room chairs with unnatural power and strength. I remember Rodd looking at me and saying, "What are you doing? Get out of the house!" I heard the fire engines coming within seconds. Firefighters began pulling their big, bulky hoses through the front door while another fireman went through the house to our attic. Soon there were firemen on the roof. The fire was put out quickly with only the east walls of the living room and master bedroom gone. The firemen had extinguished the fire before it reached the attic. Through all this, the lit Christmas tree in the living room, with opened gifts still resting under its boughs, stood grand in contrast to the ashes and smell of burnt wood, stucco, and carpet. It took more than a year to resolve the home insurance issues and retake our home.

1977, was one of the saddest years of my life. My mother asked Rodd and I to do her a favor. She asked us to fly to Detroit, Michigan, and help my older sister, Mary Helen, who was divorced by that time. She had had five children while working full-time and putting her husband through medical school, or so she thought. Her two sons lived with their father and the three girls lived with their mother. Mary Helen was drinking too much. One day the teachers at her daughters' school called the police when they noticed Mary Helen was drunk. She had picked up the children at school, and her car was weaving back and forth as they pulled out of the school parking lot and onto the street. The police came, arrested my sister, and placed the three girls in a state-run orphanage.

When we arrived in Grosse Pointe, Michigan, a suburb of Detroit, we found Mary Helen in desperate condition. She was high on drugs and alcohol living with her fiancé, Jim M. We talked with her doctors and her lawyer. They could not offer much help or guidance. We visited Mary Helen's three daughters who were being held by court order in the state's custody. They were 6, 8 and 10 years of age. So young, so vulnerable. Our attempts to help Mary Helen were unsuccessful, but we made up our mind to ask for temporary custody of my three nieces. We completed the appropriate paperwork and came home. We were told a social worker would be coming to our home to do a thorough investigation. Rodd and I gathered letters of support from our pediatrician, letters from our children's pre-school teachers, and letters from friends stating we were good people, good parents.

Once home, the drama continued. Mary Helen called and asked if she could come to our home and stay with us for a while. We said yes. Within hours of her arriving she drank every alcoholic beverage in our home, including the kirsch in the kitchen cabinet. We tried to get her to see a psychiatrist. We attempted everything we could think of to get her help. However, it was to no avail. Mary Helen called our mother and told her that Rodd and I were mistreating her and that she needed to come rescue her. Mother showed up in a matter of minutes and immediately accused Rodd and I of doing harm. Mother took hold of Mary Helen's arm to leave. As she was leaving my home, my mother said she never wanted to speak to me again. I figured this was just a reaction, so I called her two days later. She asked if I had not understood her, she never wanted to speak to me again. I cannot put in words how this affected me. I was young, trying to care for my own young children, trying to have the "perfect" family, trying to separate myself from all my families' issues, and trying to help my sister. I was crying at home but still smiling in public.

Our family was fractured and would never be the same.

Meanwhile, Mary Helen's ex-husband approached the court and said that he would take his three girls and raise them, as he already had their two brothers. He did not want Rodd and I to have the girls. He was granted custody. The girls would later tell the horrors they experienced in their father's home. Their father would later go to prison. Despite my sister working two jobs to put her husband through medical school, he never did complete medical school but rather honed his skills as a sociopath, disguised as a social worker, taking advantage of others.

My relationship with my mother was never the same after this experience. Years later I ran into her at Macy's. We spoke to each other briefly. I walked away crying. Once I saw her from a distance at Meiner's grocery in Brookside but pretended not to notice her. My children were with me. Only serious illnesses would have us speaking to each other again. Years later my mother would write to me and tell me she was sorry. I appreciated her letters, but they did not fill the void in my heart and soul. One cannot relive the years lost. I never lost the need and desire to have my mother tell me I was doing a good job, to praise me, to love my children as they grew up, and to share the excitement of my children's lives.

During this time Rodd and I continued to work as a team raising our family, supporting each other in our careers, and engaging in extracurricular activities related to our children. I was a Cub Scout Den Mother and Brownie leader. Rodd was the Cub Scout leader and spent time each summer at the Boy Scout Camp in Osceola, Missouri. No matter how busy we were, Rodd insisted we take an annual family vacation. We camped at Jellystone in the Ozarks. We camped in Minnesota and canoed the Boundary Waters between Minnesota and Canada. We vacationed in the Colorado Rocky Mountains, where we hiked and explored trails. I loved Colorado during the day but once the sun went down behind the mountains, as early as 4:00 pm, I froze. Camping in a tent was not my idea of a vacation but it was the only option we had with a young family. Rodd had grown up in Colorado and loved to camp. He hoped the joy of camping would rub off on me and the children. However, not so much. Bridget hated outhouses and preferred logs. David once connected with a family of leeches that attached themselves to his foot. Danny threw up in the tent more than once. I learned I like warm climates more than cold, I like a mattress more than a sleeping bag, and I like a drive-through more than goulash on the open fire.

Major influencers and lessons I was learning at this stage of my Life:

There are a lot of twists and turns, ups and downs, throughout life. We must learn to adapt and cope and understand that we cannot control many of the things that happen in our lives. The three most memorable memories from this period of my life are described below.

- Because of my rapid heart rate and rhythmic irregularities, I was followed by Drs. Bell and Kindred at St. Luke's Hospital. One day Dr. Bell was not available, so I saw Dr. Kindred. I will never forget the first thing he said to me, "Do you want to be sick?" I said, "No." He then said, "let's keep you well."

I learned I have some control over the way I think and feel. **I have a choice**. I wanted to be healthy.

- It was 1977 when my mother told me she never wanted to talk to me again. I figured this would only last a week or a month until she would want to see me and talk. Years passed. We never get time back.

Once again, I learned how important family is and I wanted to be **loved and accepted** by my family and others. Now, I engage myself in my children's and our grandchildren's lives and savor the moments we have together.

- When Rodd was working on his MBA, he would often share what he was studying. One class he took was Organizational Behavior, taught by Professor Miller at the University of Missouri-Kansas City. I loved this course even though I was never in the classroom. I read Rodd's classroom notes and learned so much. Like, "Words don't mean the same thing to all people"; "Words don't mean, People mean;" "Don't generalize". I learned that for real communication to occur there had to be a sender and a receiver, and the receiver must respond by acknowledging what they heard and understood. But the main lesson I learned by auditing this class through Rodd is that "People do things for people – not systems." I never received my MBA, but I learned important lessons that helped me. Rodd is a natural teacher.

I learned it's important to **share what you are learning** and **help others**, otherwise what you know may become useless or outdated.

I was also learning at this time:

I like **teaching**. You get to be an actor at times.

Words don't mean, **people mean.**

People do things for people, not systems.

The Reader's most significant memories and influences from thirty to thirty-five years of age:

Chapter 8

1980 – 1985

Martha: 35 to 40 Years of Age

I WAS YOUNG but didn't know it. I was tired most of the time, but then again, parents are usually tired. Our children needed transportation, and I was their chauffeur. I spent most of my time in the car. Every season of the year called for something: soccer practice, soccer games, football practice, football games, baseball practice, baseball games, basketball practice, basketball games. Then of course there were the post season tournaments.

There were weekly dance lessons 10 months a year with a dance recital every spring. Mildred Lyons, Bridget's dance instructor, expected each mother to make their daughter's recital costumes, usually three a year. Prior to making the costumes, each mother had to have a template of the costume made of muslin and fitted to their daughter. Once the template was approved, Mildred would give mothers the appropriate taffeta, netting, sequins, and beads. The costumes were beautiful, but challenging, original, but time consuming, sequined, with gloves, feather boas, and layers of tutus. Many mothers hired seamstresses to complete their daughter's costumes. I liked to sew and enjoyed pulling out the portable sewing machine, threading the needle and bobbin. I'd oil the foot pedal since it had been a year since I had used it. Bridget, who began dance lessons at three years of age, had dozens of costumes over the 11 years she took dance. I'm glad she has kept most costumes.

Mr. Frank Pennington was our elderly neighbor, the age I am now. His wife died shortly after we moved in next door to him in 1972. He became the back-up grandfather to tens of children on the block. Children knocked on his back door – always after 1:00 pm since he was a late sleeper - asking for "7-up and gum, please." About twice a month, Mr. Pennington joined our family for dinner. He usually brought homemade vegetable soup or New York strip steaks marinating in sauce that Rodd grilled. What a treat. Mr. Pennington knew I was tired, and the respite tasted as good as the meal itself. Once when he was over at our home, we asked him why he stayed up every night till midnight and then got up around noon the next day. He said, "Because the day is half over when I get up, and the next day is almost here." His biological family lived out of town, he was lonely, and the neighbors and children were his family.

Concurrent with my teaching position at Avila, I decided to go back to school and work toward another graduate degree. This time I worked for a Master of Arts Degree in Counseling Psychology. I realized I was more interested in caring for the psycho-social needs of others than the physiological, medical-surgical needs/conditions of patients. I also realized after teaching for six years, I could not teach in a profession like nursing without continuing to practice my clinical skills. Students in Nursing deserve teachers that are clinically proficient. To stay credible as an assistant professor in nursing I would need to take a part-time job to sustain my clinical skills. However, at the time I had three young children 9, 11, and 13 years of age and was not willing to compromise the time I had with them.

I was excited to be studying in the field of psychology. My first course was an Introduction to Counseling. I used a textbook by Gary S. Belkin. This small textbook of 400+ pages gave an overview of counseling theories and helped me compare the different approaches counselors and psychologists use to help individuals gain insight into their behaviors and proposed methodologies for changing behavior. I started out believing I was a Rogerian in my approach to working with clients, i.e., the client has the answers within themselves if given the opportunity to reflect on and explore their mental health issues in a caring and non-judgmental environment. I think most students start out in psychology leaning toward being Rogerian. But within a year I began calling myself Adlerian. Adlerian theory made much more sense to me. Adlerian believe that individuals determine their own behavior, and it is the role of the counselor to develop an understanding of the goals and lifestyle of the client and then explain the individual to him or herself and help them set new goals with a new lifestyle.[1] It was also at this time I began to understand Gestalt theory. Gestalt theory gave me a conceptual framework that helped me manage my diverse life roles. I moved my priorities, actions, and dialogue from center stage to backstage as needed or demanded by the situation.

I devoured the course work. Professor Helen Lee Stevens was remarkable. It took me three years to complete my Master of Art's degree. Many of the students in my classes shared their personal mental health issues, and I began to see a trend, i.e., students working on a degree in counseling were often there in class because of their own mental health issues. I guess you cannot help thinking about and processing your own behavior and mental health during classes. It is kind of like medical student's disease, i.e., one ends up getting or experiencing the symptoms of the disease being studied. Plus, taking counseling classes was a two-fer. It is a whole lot cheaper than paying $150 per hour for an individualized counseling session, and you are earning a college degree.

I continued taking classes after I received my M.A., hoping to complete a Ph.D. However, the stress of a full-time job, three children, and a desire to share the joys of those years convinced me to withdraw from classes. A class I will never forget was: Human Sexuality. During one class we were given blindfolds and told to spend the next 20 minutes using our sense of touch to move throughout the classroom holding each other's hands and sensing each other's emotions. Then the discussion came up about the number of sexual partners that students had had. Students openly disclosed the number of sexual partners they had over their short lives. I was the sexual conservative in the room. I don't think anyone believed me or maybe they wondered what was wrong with me when I told them I only loved one man, and for me sex came with love and marriage.

Although I worked from 1977 through 1983 at Avila, I had summers off. Teaching is a great profession for mothers with young children. During the summer months we went swimming most days at the Jewish Community Center. All the children on our block had big wheels and with our street closed to major traffic, the street became a racetrack. The children were never bored. There were the dogs, Ginny and Dolly, that chased squirrels while the children rode their big wheels and their bicycles around the banana island on our street. Their imaginations soared with their limited material resources.

We put in a new kitchen in 1981, which was a relief. After 9 years of living in our home, I got a built-in dishwasher and a trash compactor. We took memorable vacations in the 80's. In 1980 we went to see Mr. Pennington who had moved to upper Wisconsin, near Green Bay, to live with his son's family. In 1982, Rodd took three weeks off from work and we drove from Kansas City through New Mexico, Arizona, California, Nevada and Utah. We loved it. We visited the Painted Dessert, Grand Canyon, San Diego Zoo, Disneyland, the Hearst Castle, China town in San Francisco, the Golden Gate Bridge, Sausalito and anyplace along the road that looked like fun. We went back to San Diego in 1985, only this time we rested on the sand.

Although I was preparing myself to make a career change, it came sooner than I expected. I was called into the Administrative Office by the Director of the Nursing Department at Avila University and told that for financial reasons my contract for the coming academic year (1983-1984) would not be renewed. Wow! That was a blow. It hurt. I thought I was one of the best teachers on the faculty. I had even been selected that year by the college graduating class as the faculty person they would most like to address the graduation class, at their baccalaureate- ceremony. Even though I had a Master of Science Degree in Nursing, had worked on medical and surgical units at the hospital, I was young and the most recent hire. I suddenly realized some life decisions are made for us and not in sync with one's personal timeline.

I took some time off but began looking for a job by mid-summer. Although I treasured being home with my family, I wanted to use my education and further my career. Within 24 hours of interviews, I had two job offers. While I was working on my Master of Arts degree in Counseling, I did my counseling practicums at Research Medical Center (RMC), working with chronically and terminally ill patients. Following the last practicum, I wrote a job description based on the work I had been doing and asked the medical center to consider hiring me. The new position looked promising on paper with data and outcomes to support its funding. Experience had taught me that it is more satisfying to design a new position rather than fill a vacancy. I was surprised when the hospital administration called and said my proposed position for counseling chronically and terminally ill patients had been funded and I could start work. I told them I would like 24 hours to think it over. I didn't share that I had just been offered another position.

The other job offer started with my responding to a Want Ad in the Kansas City Star newspaper. In 1983, most jobs were advertised through the Newspaper. There was no such thing as the internet. The position listed was for a health-coordinator/educator within a Family Practice Residency program. The position description defined the major job responsibilities as: providing patient education, assisting with resident physician education, and managing the health care for pregnant and parenting teens enrolled in a new federally funded research program. The job description and the idea of being part of a national research initiative intrigued me.

St. Mary's Hospital Family Medicine Residency program had just been awarded a federally funded Adolescent Pregnancy and Parenting Program (TPPP) grant through the Administration of Children, Youth, and Families (ACYF), Office of Adolescent Pregnancy and Parenting (OAPP). With this grant, teen mothers and their babies would receive comprehensive health care and social services through a coordinated community effort. The goal was to demonstrate that the proposed model of care described in the federal proposal would result in improved health outcomes for a high-risk population of pregnant teens and their babies. An outside team of researchers from the University of Missouri Kansas City would be responsible for the program's evaluation.

It was quite a contrast. Work with chronically or terminally ill patients or work in a Family Practice Residency Program providing patient education and supporting the health care of young mothers and their babies. The jobs were at polar ends of life's continuum. I accepted the position at St. Mary's Hospital, Family Residency Program. We all make choices that change our life trajectory, and I had no insight into what was ahead for me.

It was quite an adjustment for everyone in the family when I took the full-time job at Saint May's Family Practice Residency. Even though I had negotiated a flexible work schedule my children were disappointed. "Can't you go back to your old job, at Avila?" was their chorus. I was tired and had less patience. Danny stopped me one night and said, "Don't yell at me. Will you go back to your old job?"

Throughout the transition, I remained hopeful that I could balance everything with my husband's help and be a good mother and a good practitioner. A close friend, Judy DiBella, drove our children home from school most afternoons during their grade school years. She made sure they got into the house safely. I also left work every day by 4 pm so I could drive after school, evening carpools. I had negotiated this as part of my job description and contract prior to accepting the position. Those early childhood years are important, and I didn't want to miss them.

Nothing was more important to me than loving and supporting our children.

My full-time position was primarily funded through the federal grant. Over the next six years I learned some critical life skills that would prepare me for what was to come.

- I learned how to apply for public and private sources of funding to support an unmet or underfunded need in the community. I learned that grants, particularly federal grants, come with regulations, performance standards, and reporting requirements. I learned that if you miss deadlines for new proposals or refunding applications, you are automatically disqualified from review and consideration.
- I learned the importance of data collection and program evaluation. I learned to track client/patient outcomes using specific criteria. I learned how to code services and document the duration and the intensity of services. I learned how to work in partnership with researchers using data to improve or redirect the services that a teen needed and would be offered. This hands-on experience was critical to my understanding the complexity and value of research and evaluation when practically translated to enhance practice.
- I learned how to write professional letters. I had never been responsible for writing professional letters in previous jobs. I was self-conscious. I would sometimes spend an hour writing and redrafting a one-page letter. I worried about the content of the letter, the spelling, and the grammar. I did not want to make a mistake. I gained confidence in my writing and began thinking more about what I wanted the letter to say rather than how to say it.
- I learned how to survive criticism and lies being spread about me in the community. There was a lot of gossip and discontent in the community when St. Mary's Hospital was awarded the Teen Pregnancy-Teen Parenting federally funded grant. Saint Mary's Hospital was a Catholic hospital administered through the sisters of Saint Mary's in Leavenworth. During the Ronald Reagan

Administration (1980-1988) grant dollars were often awarded to religiously based pro-life organizations. It did not take long before the Saint Mary's Hospital grant became known throughout the greater Kansas City community as the "Chastity Grant." No less, a Catholic (me) had been hired to manage the health care of pregnant teens.

Under this contextual cloudy claim, I was intentionally not invited to community collaborative meetings with organizations that were pro-choice. There were rumors about the program and an immediate bias against my ability to meet the needs of the young teen mothers and fathers. Even the grant partnering organizations failed to notify me of upcoming local community meetings that were held to discuss pregnant teens. When I showed up unexpectedly to meetings that I knew I should be at, I would hear the whispers, "Who invited her."

- I learned life isn't fair. In 1986, Governor John Ashcroft appointed me to the Missouri State Task Force on Adolescent Pregnancy and Parenting that met in Jefferson City once a month for eighteen months. Eunice Kennedy Shriver had put in a call to Governor Ashcroft, encouraging him to appoint me. The Task Force was charged with exploring issues related to teen pregnancy and making recommendations on how to address the issue across the state. Although there were significant religious and philosophical differences held by the members of the task force and an appearance of open mindedness to the general public's input, the Task Forces' final recommendations had been inaudibly determined before the first meeting. Life is not always fair and sometimes hard work does not pay off.
- I learned the importance of developing caring relationships. Teens want an adult in their life that they can talk with, that listens unconditionally, and acknowledges their successes, no matter how small. One teen mother of a one-year-old would often knock on my office door when she could not find me in the health clinic. One day she said, "Guess what, Martha, I'm not pregnant." I said, that's great! Then she said, "Guess what, I'm still in school." She

also had a part time job that required her to take the public bus to and from work. I got up from my chair and hugged her. I told her I was proud of her and that she was doing a great job even though it must be hard. She smiled, and I smiled.
- I learned behavioral changes take time. I was in New Haven, Connecticut, at a Teen Forum where teens from around the country talked about their experiences as a teenage parent. The purpose of the Forum was to encourage other teens to postpone having sex and the possible pregnancy that might follow. The young woman, Rachel, that I took with me from Kansas City did a beautiful job telling other teens her life story. She shared the ups and downs of being a young mother and encouraged others to complete their education before they had a child. After the event I sat next to Rachel at dinner. I told Rachel she had done an outstanding job. She looked up at me and said, "I'm starting to believe it myself." Sometimes it is easier giving advice than acting on it. It is also known that those who support and encourage others to adopt new behaviors are the ones most likely to adopt and change their own behaviors.

After a few months on the job at St. Mary's Family Practice Residency, I was told that there was going to be a federal site visit. A federal project officer, Marjorie Mecklenburg, would be checking to see if Saint Mary's Hospital, the grantee, had fully implemented the Teen Pregnancy - Parenting Program grant (TPPP) as described within the funded proposal. There would be interviews with teen parents and with the staff responsible for providing direct services to the teens across collaborating agencies. Medical records would be pulled and reviewed to see what services teens were receiving or missing. There would be interviews with the researchers from the University of Missouri-Kansas City to assure that staff were correctly documenting their interventions and that the researchers were gathering the appropriate data from the program records and staff.

When it came my turn to be interviewed, I was passionate and intense. The TPPP was responding to a major need in the community. The Federal

Project officer couldn't leave Kansas City without knowing we were doing a good job, and teens were benefiting from our services and care.

Marjory Mecklenburg, who had been appointed by President Ronald Reagan to direct the Office of Adolescent Pregnancy Programs in the United States Department of Health and Human Services met with the TPPP program team and summarized her findings from the site visit prior to returning to Washington, DC. She expressed that St. Mary's was fully implementing the federal grant and teens were receiving the comprehensive health care services described within the proposal. She told us that a positive report from the federal government would be forthcoming.

Then Marjory Mecklenburg asked to speak with me privately. After everyone else had left the conference room, she said, "Martha, Eunice Kennedy Shriver, the Executive Director of the Joseph P. Kennedy, Jr. Foundation, is looking for people like you to help her start a new initiative. May I give her your name?"

The unimaginable happened just a few weeks later. I received a personal letter from Eunice Kennedy Shriver, inviting me to submit a grant proposal on behalf of St. Mary's Hospital to become one of the first **Community of Caring** (COC) programs in the country. You may know that Eunice Kennedy Shriver and her husband, Sargent Shriver, founded the Special Olympics, launched Head Start in their backyard, and were the force behind the Peace Corp and Job Corp programs of the 1960's. This new initiative, building Communities of Caring, was to focus on improving pregnancy outcomes for young mothers and their babies and thus reduce the number of children born with special needs.

Eunice had been hospitalized at John's Hopkins Hospital on several occasions and rather than stay in bed or her hospital room, she roamed the halls of the hospital to see what was happening. Once you got to know Eunice, you would understand she was not a woman who could or would sit still. She had many irons in the fire with the intent of creating or adapting human service systems for the better. While roaming the halls of the hospital, she came upon the Adolescent Pregnancy Clinic where she learned that many pregnant teens often hide their pregnancy and only access prenatal care in their 3rd trimester. She learned that pregnant teens often don't eat well, drop out of school, and that their babies are often born too early and underweight. She was determined to change this.

In 1982, Eunice decided to design and produce a curriculum that addressed the health care and social-emotional needs of young mothers. Her initial goal was to pilot the **Community of Caring (COC)** curriculum in nine communities across the country, including rural and urban areas with diverse racial and ethnic populations, to see if the implementation of the curriculum resulted in improved pregnancy outcomes for teen mothers and their babies. Chapters within the COC curriculum were written by experts across the country, including Dr. Robert Coles, Dr. William May, and Arnold Schwarzenegger. Her national goal was to highlight the importance of early and continuous prenatal care and developmentally appropriate well-baby and well-child healthcare. Eunice Kennedy Shriver never thought small, rather took on issues of national importance. Many that knew her said that if she had only been born a male, she would have been President of the United States.

The application to become one of the nine pilot COC sites in the country had to be submitted within two weeks. Within the application, I needed to state why I thought I could join an elite group of nurses and educators and direct one of the nine proposed Community of Caring centers in the United States. The application required letters of support from the hospital administration and from community leaders. I also had to attach a budget that did not exceed $9,000. I immediately knew where to start. I made an appointment to talk with the CEO of St. Mary's hospital, Mr. William Thompson.

I walked into the CEO's office smiling and excited. I explained the opportunity and asked for help in completing the application/proposal. I described how I thought getting this new pilot program would benefit the hospital, the community, but most of all teen parents. Mr. Thompson looked up from his desk just long enough to say, "If you can't write it and manage it yourself, you don't deserve to get it." Nothing more was said. I walked out of the office.

For the next week, I worked, determined to write and submit a worthy application/proposal. In addition to what the proposal asked for, I attached my photo and described what kind of person I was, including my educational background and work experience. I wanted this grant. I wanted to become part of this effort, and I knew it was important to sell myself. I've been told by others that when someone tells me no or thinks I can't do something, I will prove them wrong. From a young age, I wanted to be successful. I had not heard the word 'over-achiever' yet, but I would understand it later in my life.

It all moved so quickly after that. I was notified that my proposal and application had been selected, and I was to arrive in Washington, D.C. within two weeks and complete an intensive 7-days of training on the **Community of Caring** curriculum and the implementation of the grant. My life was turned upside down, like an upside-down cake, I didn't see the delicious part that was coming.

This was my first trip to Washington, DC. However, over the next eight years, Washington, D.C. would become my second home. Eunice Kennedy Shriver attended every training and presentation that week, arriving early and staying to the very end. The Community of Caring (COC) training was intense. Eunice questioned, challenged, and pushed back at those presenting. She did this with purpose. She wanted those of us, who would soon be directing the COC pilot programs and representing her on a national stage, to be well prepared when others on our home turf would challenge the content and exercises within the new curriculum. She also wanted to be sure that our personal values reflected (were not in conflict with) the values rooted within the COC curriculum: Family, Caring, Responsibility, Respect, and Trust.

There were 10- and 12-hour days spent in a classroom with speakers like Bill May and Robert Coles. Eunice kept us awake during these long days by introducing us to renowned scholars and sustaining our energy with gourmet meals. There was Jambalaya, swordfish, steak, pies, cakes, pastries, and warm rolls with whipped butter. I sat in the conference room anticipating the next meal. Although many of us were putting on the pounds, Eunice never gained an ounce. She was dynamic, motivating and encouraging! She was anxious for us to breathe in the knowledge and research which was aired.

Herb Cramer, a noted publicist, teacher, and author whose writings include the motto for Special Olympics International, "Let me win, but if I cannot win, let me be brave in the attempt", took some of us on a walk-run tour of Washington, D.C. every morning at 6 am covering two to five miles of history. He was a powerful, yet humble figure as Director of Communications and assistant to the chairman of the Joseph P. Kennedy Jr. Foundation and Special Olympics International. So even from 6 to 7 am each morning, we were learning. Herb Kramer lost his mother in the Triangle Shirtwaist Factory Fire of 1911, in Greenwich, New York, and often spoke of his mother and how her death impacted his life. Although a historian and communications scholar, he understood the importance of family and the other core values of Community of Caring. Herb was there to document our engagement in the early development and trajectory of the Community of Caring. Knowing Mrs. Shriver's intensity, he wisely knew that we needed the morning exercise to survive another day in the classroom.

With Eunice, every minute counted. Each evening dinner was rich with guests. One night William (Bill) Raspberry, a Pulitzer Prize-winning columnist for the Washington Post and one of the most widely read Black Journalist of his generation, sat down and had dinner with us. Each dinner was an intimate party with only 12 or 15 people gathered around a table of food. The dialogue that informed but challenged us was our dessert.

Though the content and information presented throughout the week was exceptional, the initial values discussion made a lasting impression on me. This presentation focused on an exercise using The Life Time Line worksheet.

Using the Life Time Line form, I was asked to recall and write down three critical memories I have from each five-year period of my life. I was asked to identify who was involved in those memories and what I was feeling at the time of the experience. Then I was asked to write down the value or life lesson that emerged for me from that critical memory. Taking this exercise to the next level, I was also asked to look forward and imagine what critical memories I would make in the coming decade.

Eunice Kennedy Shriver believed that if you were going to teach from the COC curriculum, you needed to know what your values are and where they came from. If you do not know what your own values are, how can you intentionally act on them? How can you teach and model them?

Circa 1983-1990

The nine directors that had been selected to lead the Community of Caring pilot programs went back to their cities and towns and worked to implement the curriculum. Eunice would frequently visit our Kansas City site and talk directly with the teens to learn what issues they faced and what they thought could be done to improve the outcomes for young mothers and their babies. Eunice Kennedy Shriver was a persistent and driven woman who took copious notes. She was a problem solver and change agent in pursuit of excellence.

For eight years, 1983 through 1990, I worked with Eunice Kennedy Shriver, traveling across the country educating teachers and parents on the Community of Caring approach to working with teens. I am so grateful to Eunice for giving me this experience. Those eight years contributed more to my professional growth and future success than any other professional experience in my life. It was not uncommon for Eunice to call and ask me to meet her the next day to discuss public policy with legislators like her brother, Ted Kennedy from Massachusetts, or the Senator from Illinois, Paul M. Simon.

Eunice Kennedy Shriver, my mentor, taught me:

- The importance of developing professional and collegial relationships! People do things for people not systems. "Build your team," she would say. Eunice's team consisted of George Zitnay, Bob Kenny, Bob Howard, Herb Kramer, Eileen Crane, me, and many others. We traveled everywhere together. We could anticipate each other's presentations and build on what each other offered.
- How to effect change within the United States Congress. I basically got a course in Civics 101. There were trips to the Russell, Dirksen, and Hart Buildings to visit senators; trips to the Rayburn building to visit congressmen. I was able to track a legislative bill introduced in the United States Senate or the House of Representatives. I saw how staffers played a major role in negotiating and moving legislation forward. It surprised me that bills to fund health and human service programs were seldom funded as a standalone bill. Rather funding for smaller human service program efforts were often hidden within a massive infrastructure bill which no one thoroughly read. This was a common practice used by senators and representatives to have their personal interests and promises to their constituencies funded.

- How to write a grant. Eunice Kennedy Shriver asked Brian Balicki, PhD, with Health Policy Studies in 1988 to come to Kansas City, Missouri, and help me write a grant to become a Director of a Comprehensive Child Development Program (CCDP). In preparation for writing the grant, we drove through the neighborhoods documenting what we saw. We talked to families and existing organizations to better understand specific needs of families and children living in poverty. We looked for what was missing in our community. We looked at issues related to access. We looked for partnerships. This helped us with demographics and how to frame our approach to dealing with the issues. I learned how to write outcomes and adopt measures that would be used to measure progress.
- How to frame your message or narrative. When we were in New Haven, Connecticut, participating in a Teen Forum, it didn't go as well as we hoped. The press approached Mrs. Shriver afterward. She immediately went on the offense and talked about what a success our forum had been. She gave new meaning to old words and changed the narrative. This was my first experience in how to control and structure the conversation and narrative.

Eunice Kennedy Shriver spent much of her later life exploring and researching the moral development of children. Put more simply, how children learn right from wrong. The primary person she worked with at this period of her life was Robert Coles, MD. Dr. Coles, Professor of Child Psychiatry at Harvard University, who wrote in 1986, *The Moral Life of Children: How children struggle with questions of moral choice in the United States and elsewhere.* Dr. Coles is often remembered as the person who counseled Ruby Bridges during the integration of public schools in New Orleans.

I am so grateful to Mrs. Shriver for giving me the opportunity to work with her and to grow professionally and develop lifelong friends across the country.

It is amazing what you can balance and do when you enjoy what you are doing. Amid all this work and travel, Rodd asked me what I thought about him working in the country of Sudan, in the Sahara Dessert, for 6-8 weeks. I saw it as an adventure and an opportunity for him. It was a once in a lifetime experience. He would be traveling throughout Sudan to assess the financing, design, and construction of agricultural research stations. The USAID (United States Agency for International Development), the Sudanese Government, and the World Bank wanted Rodd to identify the problems and get the agricultural research stations back on track. He had to do it.

Rodd left the first of November and returned home in time for Christmas. While Rodd was away, the children and I dressed pillows in his clothes and sat his clone in the living room. Each morning, we greeted him and told him to have a good day. We heard from Rodd only a couple of times during his assignment. There were no cell towers or cell phones then. Communication was difficult. Rodd came home with hundreds of slides, stories, and very special gifts, the least of which was a hand woven red, white, and black rug 10 feet by 4 feet. It is a treasure. His trip had been a success and the Sudanese Government published and praised his efforts and achievements.

On December 6th, 1984, my mother turned 70 years old. I decided to invite her over and quietly extended the invitation to a few of her friends. I had a cake made for her. It read "Happy 70th Birthday". When my mother came through the front door to cries of "Surprise", she was shocked to see her friends and even more shocked at the cake. She immediately ran toward the cake and using her thumb and forefinger wiped out her age on the birthday cake adding "my daughter has her dates mixed up." Mother had lied about her age. I do too, sometimes.

I have always been competitive. I wanted to be the best speller in grade school. I loved math competitions. I strived for good grades. I represented Greenland at a mock United Nations meeting and had Greenland playing a significant role in the world's economy. Unlikely. This desire to be the best, to be successful, was passed along to our children. As parents, we instilled in them the desire to excel whether in academics or sports. We wanted them to have a sense of pride and to believe in themselves.

There is no better example of this than the grade school Science Fair competitions at Saint Elizabeth's grade school, in 1984. When David was in 8th grade, Danny in 6th grade, and Bridget in 5th grade, they each took first place in their science class projects. Listed below are each of their hypotheses.

- David's science project hypothesis: "How to stimulate the endogenous production of endorphins and thus reduce pain without the use of addicting drugs."
- Danny's science project hypothesis: "Listening to classical music will reduce your blood pressure and lower your pulse."
- Bridget's science project hypothesis: "Classmates that engage in extracurricular sports and activities will have a lower percentage of body fat than those who do not."

Of course, I helped our children learn how to use blood pressure cuffs and calipers. I helped them research their areas of interest and helped them sign up research subjects whose parents signed consent forms. Rodd helped them design their posters and construct their displays. All three of our children proved their hypothesis. I laugh about this now. Such big ideas. But isn't that what children need? Someone who cares about them, someone who will work with them, someone who wants them to succeed in life, and someone who sets high expectations for them. An untoward outcome of this science fair contest was that other parents at the school became more engaged in their child's science project. Sometimes a little competition can spur greater creativity and there were those that didn't want the Staker children taking the first-place ribbons again.

David was spending the night at his best friend, Michael Nauman's, home. The phone rang. Michael Nauman's mother, Carol, picked up the phone. A classmate of David's, Kate, was calling to talk with him. Carol called upstairs to David and told him he had a call. Before Carol could hang up, she heard Kate exclaim. "David, your mother is on TV talking about sex." Everything went quiet. Carol knew she couldn't hang up the phone at this point, so she continued to listen. After what seemed like a long pause,

David said, "Kate, call me if she makes any mistakes," and then hung up the phone. David never mentioned this phone call to me.

David excelled in basketball and was starting guard for the Rockhurst High School team that won the Missouri State Basketball championship in 1987. Danny excelled in Journalism, winning state awards for his publications. He received the "R" award for his leadership at Rockhurst High School. Bridget engaged in track, volleyball, and basketball and loved distance running. However, her first love was dance. Mildred Lyons would often remind Bridget how well she performed. Bridget earned her "toe shoes" before retiring and turning to sports, which was the publicly assumed choice for a 5'10" beauty.

My greatest fear at this time in my life was that I would forget to pick up a child at school, at a friend's home, or at practice. I would dream about this. It was a constant worry.

I had heard about a book, *Maggie's American Dream* by James Comer, and read it because James Comer was born to a mother who was an immigrant, without resources, and had become well educated and successful. It was a beautiful story, and I loved it. It started me thinking about my own ancestry and the hardships my grandparents experienced. I began to appreciate and understand more about the generations that preceded me. I began to understand slavery and discrimination. It expanded my world.

Friends were an important part of my life. Most of our friends were parents of our children's friends. It is a natural extension as you raise a family. One of my best friends was, and is, Carol Nauman. Carol loved antiques and didn't confine her search for the perfect piece of depression glass or that special ladder-back chair she needed in her new home. We would travel to Leavenworth, Kansas, or Clinton, Missouri. Once when I was out with Carol, near the Missouri River, I found six Waterford crystal white wine glasses with the original green Waterford stickers still on them. They had never been used. They were all in one box and for sale, $7.98. I approached the owner and asked if it was $7.98 for each wine stem or $7.98 for the box of six. He said it was for a box of six. One Waterford wine glass at the time was $68.00. I got a $408.00 value for $7.98. It just happened that the

Lismore pattern of the wine glasses was a match to my Waterford Crystal at home.

---

1. Hansen, James C., et al. *Counseling: Theory and Process.* Second ed., Allyn and Bacon, Inc, 1977.

Major influencers and lessons I was learning at this stage of my life:

This was one of the most exciting times in my life. I was traveling, meeting people I had read about in newspapers, and I was happy. The following are the three most memorable memories from this period of my life.

- As I drove into the driveway with groceries filling the back of the station wagon, I saw David shooting baskets. He had used duct tape to make a three-point line on the driveway court. David loved shooting the basketball from behind the three-point line. I was busy carrying sacks of groceries into the house when David yelled at me, "Mom, stop and watch me. If I make this basket, I am going to be a millionaire when I grow up". I set down the groceries and stopped everything to watch. David lined up, bounced the ball once, and threw it up. It hit the rim and bounced off. I started back into the house. David said, "Wait mom, don't go inside. If I make this shot, I am going to be a billionaire when I grow up." He bounced the basketball once and leaned into the shot. Whoosh! All net. With a big smile, David said, "Mom, see I just didn't think big enough the first time.

I learned the importance of **thinking big and setting high expectations** for yourself.

- It was Thanksgiving Day in 1980. We were at Rodd's parents' home, sitting at the dining room table enjoying turkey, dressing, and mashed potatoes. My sister-in-law, Jeanie, who was a teacher in the Park Hill School District, began telling us about the the students in her fourth-grade classroom. Suddenly, David said, "Aunt Jeanie, you teach fourth grade? Aunt Jeanie answered. "Yes, David. I thought you knew that". David replied in all sincerity, "But, Aunt Jeanie, I am in fourth grade. Give me the answers."

I learned that our children thought there was a set of answers to life. It was time to share that **there is no one set of answers** and we each must study and learn to find our own answers.

- In working with young mothers who were either pregnant or parenting, I used specific lesson plans from the Community of Caring Curriculum. One day I decided to teach a module on budgeting. However, rather than teach it in a classroom I decided to take six young mothers and their babies to the Kansas City Zoo for a picnic. My daughter, Bridget, came with me to help care for the infants. Most of the young mothers had never visited the Kansas City Zoo in Swope Park. We had a picnic lunch followed by a lesson on budgeting. The lesson plan included a worksheet where teens listed their assets, debits, and monthly living expenses. The young mothers then shared their worksheets. One teen was eager to share. At the top of her asset list, she had the name of her baby boy. Her baby was her greatest asset. There were no other assets listed. All the teens agreed with her and quickly added that to their worksheet. It was the first time I had seen a baby listed on a budget sheet as an asset. But – she was right. Her baby was her greatest asset. I learned something about the way young mothers think and feel about their babies.

I learned **children are our greatest asset.**

I was also learning at this time:

Work hard and do your best. You never know who's looking and watching you. You never know what life is preparing you for. **Be ready.**

Be Alert. Life offers opportunities if you are alert and recognize them and take advantage of them.

Developmental readiness is not based just on one's physical size but on their language, social and emotional development as well.

Friendships and developing a social network are important to a healthy lifestyle.

Getting older is hard and lonely for some.

The Reader's most significant memories and influencers from thirty-five to forty years of age:

Chapter 9

1985 to 1990

Martha: 40 to 45 Years of Age

As I continued my career working with young mothers and fathers, I became more immersed with the Joseph P. Kennedy, Jr. Foundation. I became part of a trusted national team of professionals that Mrs. Shriver counted on to provide training and technical assistance to Community of Caring start-up programs across the country. In addition to helping individual schools, the team planned and presented summer conferences at the University of Virginia, the University of Colorado, and various other universities throughout the Unites States.

In 1986, Eunice Kennedy Shriver asked me to represent her in a discussion on teen pregnancy that would be broadcast live on NBC's Today Show. I arrived in New York the night before the broadcast and stayed at the Park Plaza Hotel. An NBC chauffeur picked me up early the next day and took me and a professor from the University of Michigan, the guest I was paired with, to the NBC studio. We didn't talk to each other in the car. Both of us appeared nervous. Once in the studio, I was immediately ushered into make-up where color was added to my already flushed cheeks and my hair combed and sprayed. I wore a conservative oatmeal colored two-piece suit having been warned not to wear any geometric patterned clothing. Deborah Norville, an NBC anchor, would be conducting the interview.

Once on the set, Ms. Norville introduced both the professor and me quickly and immediately engaged in the topic of teen pregnancy. After some soft preliminary questions, she went to the heart of the matter, "Should pregnant teens marry the baby's father?" The Professor from Michigan had completed research suggesting that teen mothers and their babies had a better outcome if the mother was married to the baby's father. When Ms. Norville asked me what I thought about that, I responded by saying "80% of teen marriages end in divorce." The 4- or 5-minute segment ended abruptly. I had the last word. We were quickly escorted off the studio floor to the waiting room where the chauffeur offered to take us both back to the hotel. The professor refused the ride and would not speak to me. I got in the limousine and felt terrible. I guessed the professor expected me to agree with his research. Eunice Kennedy Shriver had not told or advised me what to say prior to the broadcast. I said what I had experienced and researched. The three-hour flight back to Kansas City was awful as I continued to replay the interview in my brain. Weeks later, Eunice Kennedy Shriver said to me, "it's harder than it looks, isn't it"? Meaning being interviewed on live TV. I agreed. Later I thought, maybe Mrs. Shriver knew what needed to be said but didn't want to be the one to deliver the truth.

Mrs. Shriver nominated me to attend the Intensive Bioethics Course XIII from May 31 – June 6th, 1987, at Georgetown University. Living on the campus for the week gave me a feeling of what it might be like to live in Washington, DC. I could walk everywhere in the district and found some small local restaurants that I frequented. The course was an in-depth study of ethical theory and principles as applied to health care and biomedical research. Subject matter included content on ethical decision making, justice, beneficence, autonomy, virtues, care of the aging, gene therapy, death and dying, the allocation of health services, bioethics and the law. This course would prove helpful as I grew in my understanding and practice caring for others.

I traveled several times a month. Every time I got in a plane and fastened my seat belt, I thought "What am I doing. Why aren't I home with the kids?" I certainly had mixed feelings as a young mother. Once when I was going to miss my son's birthday, Eunice wrote to Danny and thanked him for sharing his mother. She told him I was doing important work. It was at this time that Mrs. Shriver asked me to move to Washington, D.C., and work for the Foundation. Rodd and I seriously considered it for several weeks and then decided it would not be a good move for our family.

Community of Caring

1350 New York Avenue, N.W., Suite 500
Washington, D.C. 20005-4709
202-393-1250

Eunice Kennedy Shriver
President

Herbert J. Kramer, Ph.D.
George A. Zitnay
Program Directors

DIRECTORS
Robert N. Bellah
Honorable Lindy Boggs
Robert Coles, M.D.
Robert E. Cooke, M.D.
John Dow, Jr., Ph.D.
Rev. Lois Gatchell
Janet Hardy, M.D.
Ruth Herman
Honorable Bill Honig
W. N. Kirby, Ph.D.
David Maranville
Lorraine Nadelman, Ph.D.
Lulu Mae Nix, Ed.D.
Joseph Reimer, Ph.D.
Timothy Shriver
William Sullivan, Ph.D.
Kathleen Kennedy Townsend

COMMUNITY OF CARING
REGIONAL TRAINING AND
RESOURCE CENTERS
Mency Anderson, MSW
Houston, Texas
Frances Jackson, M.N.
Elkins, West Virginia
Maureen Joyce, R.S.M.
Albany, New York
Martha Staker
Kansas City, Missouri
Frances Troutman, M.S.
Boston, Massachusetts

April 14, 1987

Mr. Daniel C. Staker
646 West 70th Street
Kansas City, MO 64113

Dear Dan:

The Community of Caring Conference held today in Washington, D.C., I am told was a success. We owe much of that success to your mother. I am sure she has told you a great deal about the Community of Caring and our efforts to carry our message to many more individuals. Your mother's efforts have helped us a lot. Her contributions today benefitted everyone at the Conference.

Thank you so much for sharing your mother with us on your birthday. Your contribution to the program is important too!

Best wishes for a very happy birthday!

Sincerely,

Eunice Kennedy Shriver

Community of Caring, Inc., Created by The Joseph P. Kennedy, Jr. Foundation

---

Between 1986 and 1988 I served on the Missouri State Task Force on Unwed Adolescent Pregnancy appointed by Governor Ashcroft. The task force met monthly in Jefferson City, Missouri. It was during this time that I started to experience a sharp pain in my neck when I turned my head to the right. Then the shooting pain in my neck began to occur sporadically without cause. An MRI with contrast showed a tumor at cervical spine, 2-3. The MRI revealed a benign neurofibroma. A neurofibroma is usually not a problem. However, this tumor was attached to the spinal cord and the vertebral artery (which carries blood to the brain). Surgery was scheduled. The hospital chaplain counseled my husband to be sure and bring the children to the hospital the morning of the surgery. The surgery was serious, and the chaplain thought the family should be together. Dr. Robert Morantz, neurosurgeon, performed the operation on Tuesday morning, March 8th, 1988. The surgery was a success, but it took more than 3 years to recover from the pain associated with it. I never feared the surgery or doubted the outcome. Perhaps it was denial, however, I believe my faith pulled me through. I believe in prayer, and lots of people were praying for me that day. But afterwards, with such a prolonged recovery, I doubted my faith. I was angry. I felt like giving up. How could God let me go through this? What was God's plan for me. At my deepest and darkest moment, I started to improve. I told myself that I would never doubt God again. He had plans for me and this was part of the journey. I continued working throughout this time. I have always found work to be therapeutic and I could still smile.

During this difficult time, the children were old enough to be primarily self-sufficient. They had learned to do their own laundry because they were tired of me mixing up and losing their clothes. David had a car and drove Danny and himself to and from school every day. Bridget was 15 and helped with meals. I remember Bridget coming to the hospital and shaving my legs since I couldn't bend my neck. Throughout this illness Sue Stephenson coordinated friends and neighbors who brought nightly meals for over a month. Sue is an angel who has already earned her wings! Rodd led the recovery team, continually reminding everyone to, "cope and deal."

A year later, in May 1989, I decided it was time to change jobs. Prior to looking for a new job, I took the summer off. I was anxious to spend more time with our children. David was in college; Danny would be a Senior at Rockhurst High School and Bridget was a Junior at St. Teresa's Academy. That summer I was hired as a consultant for the Ewing Marion Kauffman Foundation to help them gain an understanding of a new federal initiative called the Comprehensive Child Development Program (CCDP). I researched the initiative and wrote recommendations for implementing a similar program in Kansas City, Missouri. Prior to completing the assignment, I was invited to apply for the position that would direct the effort for the Kauffman Foundation.

I was interviewed by Mr. Ewing Kauffman. I sat across from him in his beautiful office, and he asked me about my work history. He was more interested in the type of person I was than in my credentials. He asked me how old I was, and I told him, "I am 43, but feel like 36." He laughed and thought that was great. I didn't get the job. When I asked why, my contact with the Foundation took me to lunch and in so many words said it was because I was a woman and wasn't a good fit with the leadership team. I was told bluntly that it wasn't Mr. Kauffman that made the decision.

However, my knowledge of the CCDP initiative availed me of an even better opportunity. I can say that now looking back. The University of Kansas Medical Center (KUMC) had just been awarded one of the 16 Comprehensive Child Development Program federal grants designed to serve young children and their families in Kansas City, Kansas. The Medical Center would call their new CCDP program, Project EAGLE. EAGLE stood for Early Action Guidance Leading to Empowerment. I was asked by Joe Hollowell M.D., the Director of the Child Development Unit at KUMC, to apply for the Assistant Director position. I took the job and started there in January of 1990. I became part of a national initiative, funded through the Administration of Children and Families.

From the onset, I understood that this program would be tracked by researchers for 5 years to determine its impact on children and families. The research question was "When pregnant women, young children, and their families - who live below the federal poverty guidelines and in vulnerable communities - receive comprehensive health care (including prenatal care), parenting education, early childhood education and family support services - are the children able to enter school prepared to learn and compete with children from more advantaged backgrounds". The services for the children and families would be delivered through home-based and center-based program options.

There was both an outside evaluation managed by Abt, Associates and an internal qualitative study done by CSR, Inc. Two things made this initiative different. First, it was a multi-generational approach to addressing poverty and school readiness. Everyone living in the home who interacted with the young focus child could receive services. Grandparents, parents, even aunts and uncles who helped care for the child or children were eligible to receive services. Second, one agency would be offering and coordinating wrap-around services for the whole family. Historically social services have been offered in isolation, like silos, with one social service agency not knowing what other social service agencies were offering the same family. Funding was built into the grant assuring that CCDP programs could offer wrap around services either through interagency agreements with existing agencies in the community or by generating the services needed. The point was that we were not to duplicate services within the given community, rather be more efficient and careful with spending federal dollars.

I was hired as Assistant Director but advanced quickly. In less than six months I became the acting Director of the Program, and Director within the first year. With time, I became the Principal Investigator, for the University of Kansas Medical Center, managing grants totaling 6-8 million dollars annually that supported young children and their families. The last 10 years at KUMC I ranked 2nd and 3rd in bringing in the most research money for the University of Kansas Medical Center. I've spent time emphasizing this career choice because it became my life's work. I loved my job and worked 23 years building Project EAGLE and raising $16 million dollars to build a new multi-tenant building where agencies would co-locate to assure children and families living in poverty received the services they needed, under one roof, at their time of need. Another thing I know now looking back, the first 16 CCDP's were the prototype for what Head Start would later call, Early Head Start. Early Head Start supports pregnant women and children from birth through the first three years of their life. The initial 16 CCDP programs/sites helped create and define Early Head Start regulations and prototypes for millions of children and families. I got to be part of this exciting development.

Starting a new job is difficult and my rise within the University of Kansas Medical Center was not easy. No one at the University of Kansas Medical Center knew what I was capable of. No one knew my history. No one had ever heard of me. No one cared. I had to learn quickly, and I had to inspire staff. Initially 16 people worked under me. I quickly learned new terminology, not necessarily new skills. I learned about Individualized

Family Support Plans (IFSP's), a Family Strengths framework, Social Capital, Ethnographic/Qualitative Research and Quantitative Research efforts using randomized trials. I was new to the University system. I was new to Kansas City. Kansas. I had to understand federal regulations and make sure we met them. There were semi-annual reports I needed to write documenting our successes and addressing our needs for improvement. My background in Nursing, managing a federal grant for teens, and having been on a national stage with the Joseph P. Kennedy Jr., Foundation, Jr. had prepared me for this.

If this had not been enough, a few individuals in the Kansas City, Kansas, community were angry that a white woman was directing this multi-million-dollar investment earmarked for young children and families living in poverty in the urban core. My life was threatened. My husband received letters in the mail with messages formed by words cut from the local newspaper. Messages threatening my life informed my husband that I was going to be in a bad accident and not make it back from a flight I was on. Since the mailed letters crossed the state line, the FBI got involved. Although the people were quickly identified and confronted by the FBI, no charges were filed. It was a very hard first year. It was also an expensive year for me, as I had to hire my own attorney. Many colleagues advised me to quit while I was ahead and get out while I could, but I never thought of quitting. I have never given up on anything I believed in. I also kept telling myself who could do this job better than me. I really believed I had what it took to make this effort successful in a community where there was such a great need. I trusted myself and never thought about failure.

Good things happened in 1990 as well. The Jones Store was a large department store with a long history of retail services in the Kansas City Metropolitan area. Annually, Jones Store sponsored through its business club a Career Day where a distinguished woman from the local community was honored as the Career Woman of the Year. A national guest speaker highlighted the program and delivered the keynote presentation. In 1990 I was Kansas City's Career Woman of the Year and Helen Gurley Brown, Editor-in-Chief of Cosmopolitan Magazine, gave the keynote address. I was nominated by colleagues from my previous job, Linda Hawley and Shirley Goode, and others that had worked alongside me as I cared for teen parents and traveled across the country with Joseph P. Kennedy, Jr. Foundation. There were letters of support for my nomination from individuals like Eunice Kennedy Shriver, and Brian Balicki, from the Health Policy Studies in Maryland. There were also letters of support from my local friends like Betsy Graham Rushton whom I met in kindergarten. Life is a mix of good and bad experiences. It's important to recognize that and appreciate the good times and grow from the bad times.

The following Martin Luther King's quotation is a favorite of my husband's. "The ultimate measure of a man is not where he stands in moments of *comfort a*nd *convenience* but where he stands at times of *challenge* and *controversy.* "

Our lives build on our experiences. What we do in kindergarten and who we play with in kindergarten influences who we become.

Martha and Rodd with Helen Gurley Brown, 1990.

Major influencers and lessons I was learning at this stage of my life:

My career began to take more of my time as our children became more independent, but my thoughts were never far from them and what they were doing. The three memories from this period of my life, 40 to 45 years of age, that I frequently recall and influenced me are described below.

- Allen Smith, a federal project officer overseeing the implementation of the Comprehensive Child Development Program (CCDP), came to visit Project EAGLE the summer of 1990. That tells you something right off. The University of Kansas Medical Center's (KUMC) CCDP program, funded for less than one year, was failing. Families had not been enrolled in the research program and services had not been delivered. The initial woman hired to direct the program resigned, and I was asked to take the leadership role, directing the nationally funded multi-million-dollar research program.

Mr. Smith said that "Unless you turn this program around in 6 weeks, I am taking the grant dollars away." The KUMC leadership were not sure if I had the skills and knowledge to resurrect the grant but gave me 6 months to demonstrate whether I could direct and manage what was then a multi-million-dollar grant for 5 years to enhance the growth and development of young children 0-5 years of age living in poverty. It seems like I was always being challenged. My major job was to motivate and educate the staff. I needed the staff to understand the intent of the grant, to recruit and enroll families, and to provide home-based services. The KUMC CCDP would within a few years become one of the outstanding research projects in the country at improving the outcomes of children and families living in poverty.

I learned to **have faith in myself** and **never give up on something I believed in**.

- As the 1990 Career Woman of the Year in Kansas City, I was to address the attendees at the annual dinner. There were more than 1000 guests packed into the Westin Crown Center ballroom. Helen Gurley Brown spoke first. After her presentation she took a few questions from the audience. One specifically addressed her recent publication on oral sex. The audience went wild and was still gnawing on the salacious topic when the Master of Ceremonies went to the podium and introduced me. I did not reference Ms. Brown's address but went to my prepared speech. I was able to get the attendees' attention immediately because I told personal stories about my life experiences and about the people who had made a difference in my life, none richer than the story Grandma Didi told me about "Making Your Hay While the Sun Shines".

I learned it is best to stick to your prepared remarks. **Don't let someone or something change what you had planned to say.**

- I had mixed feelings about traveling and being away from my family. Before leaving on a trip, I prepared enough frozen meals for the nights I would be away. I made sure all the laundry was caught up and everyone had what they needed for the next few days or weeks. And, I always had Rodd's support. He would say, "Everything will be ok. I am here and the kids and I will be fine. Go ahead. I believe in what you are doing." I realized then and even more now how blessed I was to have married the right man. We never competed, rather we supported each other.

I learned **marriage is** when two people who love each other, respect each other, and help each other grow and reach their goals. Marriage is not static but constantly changing. Our **roles change over time.**

I was also learning at this time:

Success is never guaranteed. **Enjoy small and big successes!**

Sometimes we must **prove ourselves over and over** for people to see our strengths and capabilities.

Sexism and Racism have no boundaries. Everyone is subject to it.

The Reader's most significant memories and influencers from forty to forty-five years of age.

Chapter 10

1990 to 1995

Martha: 45 to 50 Years of Age

BETWEEN 1992 AND 1995 our 3 children graduated from the University of Kansas. David graduated with an undergraduate degree in Business and then continued at KU to get a law degree. Meanwhile, Bridget graduated with a degree in accounting and continued her education at the University of Missouri Kansas City, receiving a Master of Science degree in Business with an emphasis on Tax Accounting. Danny graduated from KU with a degree in Civil Engineering and went to work. Danny has always worked and always given 100% of his attention and energy to whatever he was doing. When he wanted or needed something he went to work to earn the money. He started his own lawn mowing business in high school called "Fresh Cut," mowing more than 100 yards a week one summer. When Danny was in grade school, his dad and I gave him a framed picture of Einstein because we thought of him as "our" Einstein. We will never forget him playing Romeo in Shakespeare's Romeo and Juliet in 8th grade. He memorized the entire Shakespearian play. We knew then he had a photographic memory.

Looking back, I did a poor job preparing our children for college. Oh, they had a good education and the clothes and food they needed but I never did directly address the depth of issues facing all young adults: drugs, sex, and peer pressure. I am not sure why I didn't do a better job on this. I know I trusted our children. I rationalized that the children saw how their mother and father lived, worked, and played. As parents, we shared our values with our children. We tried to be role models for them. However, this is only part of what they needed. The more you can tell your child, share with your child one on one, the better. It is important to be very intentional when setting expectations with your child. I would do it differently if I could do it over. I am grateful our children made it through their teens. I have always believed in the goodness of people without recognizing that there are mean and angry people in the world with bad intentions. When you have been raised in a caring family where there is more good than bad, you may think everyone is a good person and has your best interests at heart. When you realize this is not the case it can be difficult. One needs more than one's values; they need to know how to use words and actions to protect themselves from harm.

David, Danny, and Bridget throughout the years

1976

1980

1995

With our children concentrating on their graduate studies and their first professional jobs, I spent most of my days and at least part of each weekend working. I was able to immerse myself in work and fully implement the Comprehensive Child Development Program (CCDP), for the University of Kansas Medical Center. The funded proposal proposed a peer-to-peer model of interventions to help families living in poverty. The staff we hired were high school graduates that had pulled themselves up by the bootstraps. The first hurdle was providing the peer models with training that focused on documentation. Since this was a research grant, documenting and recording the services and intensity of the services that families received was critical. We wanted to know what services were most helpful to families as they became more self-sufficient; which interventions were most helpful to parents in their role as the primary care giver of their children; and were the children from disadvantaged backgrounds whose families received intensive and comprehensive services over a three-to-five-year period, entering school ready to learn and able to compete with children from more advantaged backgrounds?

Initially, staff turnover was a huge issue. The first year, staff threatened to quit if I didn't give them a pay raise. I agreed that they deserved more money. The initial annual salaries averaged $13,000. I raised everyone's pay by $3,000. Within months the staff that were trained and implementing our peer model of services threatened to quit again. This time I said, ok. Quit. No one did. Over time it became apparent that it was critical to hire frontline staff that had a college degree and experience in either early childhood education and/or social work. The peer-to-peer model did not result in improved outcomes. Once the program model was revised using professional teachers and social workers, Project EAGLE became more successful.

There are only a few experiences in our life that we look back on and say had a major impact on our professional career The Head Start Management Fellows Program at the University of California Los Angeles within the Anderson School of Business and working side by side with Helen Taylor, Director of the Office of Head Start in Washington, D.C., were two major influencers on my career. I was nominated to attend the Head Start Management Fellows Program at UCLA from June 18th through June 30th, 1995. There were 12 days of intensive education across various fields of study. At the end of the course my fellow colleagues, about 30 of us, from across the country voted me the recipient of the Helen Taylor award. This is the highest award presented at the end of the Fellowship. I was asked to give the graduation address. Not only had I had grown from this experience, I became known by my peers across the country and would be tapped for future opportunities by the Office of Head Start. Incidentally, I experienced my first earthquake while in Los Angeles. It woke me one morning at 5:00 am.

I am grateful for the opportunity to be part of the Head Start family and to have worked with so many strong and capable people. Prior to this Fellowship I wasn't sure I was a good fit for the Head Start family. Some of my experiences with Head Start programs had been anything but positive, but this fellowship changed my mind. I was introduced to the upcoming leaders in the field of early education who would write the new Early Head Start legislation, regulations, and performance standards for the country.

One of the major assignments during the Johnson and Johnson Fellows program was to write a MIP: a Management Improvement Plan. This Plan was to utilize the knowledge I had gained from the UCLA business school's rigorous curriculum to improve my local Head Start/Early Head Start program. The MIP was to be a three-to-five-year plan, and I would report back on my successes and failures. My initial plan was to raise $100,000 to strengthen Project EAGLE and assure its sustainability. However, years later I would report back that I had built a $16 million-dollar multi-tenant building with public -private funding. The building called the Children's Campus of Kansas City, offered young children, birth to five years of age, and their family's early childhood education and family support services under one roof. The MIP encouraged me to think bigger and outside the box.

Although at the time this was a big deal, I now look back and see it in perspective. There were a lot of other things that happened during this time that had a major influence on my personal life. Rodd who was raised Methodist became a Catholic. Rodd had always gone to Sunday mass with me and our children, fulfilling his promise to raise our children as Catholic. Then out of the blue, he announced that he wanted to become a Catholic and participate in the sacraments. We had been married for 22 years and our children were practically grown. Why now? Rodd told me that several things influenced his decision. As he traveled for work within and outside of the United States, he would attend the local Catholic Mass. He began to recognize that the Mass was celebrated the same throughout the world. He liked the rituals and ceremony. He was also influenced by the Jesuit priests that taught our sons at Rockhurst High School. He saw the sacrifices that priest make and was inspired by their mission. And the other thing – the priest at our church, from time to time, asked him if he would like to become a Catholic. Sometimes we forget the most obvious. I had never asked Rodd to become Catholic because I always felt he was a better person than me. I need to remember "the ask".

As an adult, I never got the flu or minor illnesses. No, it was always something bigger and worse. In 1993, I needed rotator cuff surgery. I had surgery over the Christmas Holidays. It's like having a root canal the day before Thanksgiving. No fun. Later I would have two additional shoulder surgeries. In 2011 I had rotator cuff surgery and then in 2017 a shoulder replacement.

It was also during this time that the great flood of 1993 occurred, flooding parts of Kansas and Missouri. There were homes destroyed, lives lost, and economic disasters. Although the flood had no impact on my life, it flooded and hurt some of the families our program was supporting.

Rodd and I had no extra money. Most of our money between 1983 and 1995 went to pay for our children's Catholic High School education and their undergraduate studies at the University of Kansas. We never questioned this. Education for our children was our number one priority. I must admit I often found myself wishing I could buy some new furniture and a new car. However, we were still able to take family vacations, which were another priority of ours. Once when Rodd was very busy at work, he hesitated to take a vacation. His boss told him "Your children are only young once, take a vacation."

Major influencers and lessons I was learning at this stage of my life:

I am making an exception during this period of my life to record four critical memories! You will understand my need to do this as you read on.

I am aware of three different times my guardian angel was there to care for me:

- As part of his military service in the Navy, Rodd's ship visited Japan several times. While there he purchased and surprised me with a gift of Mikimoto pearls and earrings. They were beautiful. I wore the earrings almost every day to work and to social gatherings. After many years I lost one of the earrings. I thought I must have lost it at work. I looked for days and finally gave up. Then a few days later I went into my office and the missing earring was on the floor right in front of my office chair. It was out in the open. Who had placed it there?
- I Lost my grandfather's jade stick pin. It was my grandfather's favorite possession. After his death my mother gave it to me. I looked everywhere for it. Many days later I found it under the floor mat on the driver's side of the car. I cannot believe it was there and still in perfect condition. How did I find it hidden beneath the floor mat?
- It was a snowy winter evening, and I was on Interstate 70 headed home from work. It was cold and the streets were slick. I had my blinker on to take the 7th Street exit ramp, but the steering wheel wouldn't turn. I was going to go off the road. I felt someone else take over the steering wheel and keep the car on the road. I clearly felt someone's hands on the wheel.

I learned that **my guardian angel is real and there for me.** I have no doubts about this. I learned that keepsakes are very important to me, and it is important to hold them close.

- During an informal chat, Helen Taylor, Director of the Office of Head Start, told a small group of us that she had a difficult decision to make. In the upcoming Federal Early Head Start refunding package, there would be an increase in federal dollars. She was debating whether to expand the number of Early Head Start programs in the country or use the money to improve the quality of the existing Early Head Start programs. Early Head Start programs were still in their infancy, and the quality and implementation of the Early Head Start programs across the country was poor. There was a desperate need for quality improvements. However, there were thousands of young children living in poverty that had no early education or early intervention services to help with developmental disabilities.

Helen Taylor decided to fund hundreds of more Early Head Start sites. Helen Taylor died prematurely of cancer, but she had assured that Early Head Start would survive and continue to be funded. She knew the quality of program services would follow. Science was already acknowledging the importance of the early years, and this new funding would expand the number of young children, birth to three years of age, eligible to receive early education and would identify more children with developmental disabilities earlier in life so they received the early intervention services they needed.

I learned how **some decisions are hard** to make but we gather input and **do the best we can at the time.**

- With most of our money going toward college tuition, we didn't have money to buy me a newer car. So, my mother-in-law offered me her 9-year-old gold, four-door, 1986 Cutlass Oldsmobile that just happened to have a tan vinyl roof. One day I ran into a former student of mine who had recently seen me driving the car down Brookside Boulevard. She said, "I am surprised to see you driving that old car". Her intonation said, "I thought you, career woman of the year, would be driving something better than that."

I learned that **you shouldn't judge one's success by the car they drive and the clothes they wear.**

- One day at work I attended a meeting at the Reardon Convention Center which was just across the street from where I worked. I had to leave the meeting early, so I quietly got up and exited the side door. Once outside the room a woman in her middle years that worked with Black Adoption Services came running after me. She said, "I just want to thank you. You have been nice to me." I don't even remember what I said. I had worked with her briefly on occasions but did not know her well. I hurried off to my next meeting. Several weeks later I heard that she had committed suicide. I have never forgotten this. I guess we never know what is really going on with another. I wish I had. I wish I had taken more time.

Listen carefully to what others are saying and don't be afraid to ask them if everything is ok. There is nothing more important than people.

I was also learning at this time:

Be intentional and detailed when trying to teach others, especially your children.

If something isn't working, **change** what you are doing. Try something else.

Continuing education is important and can change the way you think about certain issues.

The reader's most significant memories and influencers from forty-five to fifty years of age:

Chapter 11

1995-2000

Martha: 50 to 55 Years of Age

BETWEEN 50 AND 55 years of age I grew personally and professionally. Professionally, I gained confidence in myself and stopped biting my fingernails for the first time in my life. However, by the end of the 90's, I was bored, frustrated, and restless. I had done as much as I could with the federal and local resources I could access. I had built a federally funded program to address the needs of children growing up in poverty. I had spent 10 years helping children and families succeed in school and life. I had built a team of qualified professional staff, and a diverse base of funding which would underwrite the program's sustainability for the community that valued it. I had worked within the community harnessing resources, writing interagency agreements, pulling people together, and understanding how to use program data to improve family outcomes. I understood the value of sharing data with parents, and I even went so far as to write a major report for the Unified Government on the current systems of care in Wyandotte County-Kansas City Kansas.

Then it hit me. There were resources in the community that families didn't know existed, but even when they did, they had a difficult time accessing them. Families living in poverty accepted poor quality babysitting rather than quality childcare for their child because it was all they could afford or available in their neighborhoods. There were other problems, too. Families on Medicaid with more than two children had to make multiple appointments and trips to see their pediatrician or family practice physician for their child's well-baby and well-child check-ups. Since Medicaid reimbursements compensated physicians less than private insurance companies, pediatricians limited the number of Medicaid patients they would see in one family each day. Parents might need to make multiple trips to the health clinic if they had more than two children. Complicating this might be the need to travel to another location to have their child's blood drawn for routine lab work.

Many mothers and fathers delayed getting their child evaluated for developmental concerns. Parents couldn't bring themselves to think that their child – the child they birthed – might have special needs. Parents put off appointments saying that every child is different, and let's take a wait and see approach. This delayed early intervention services that might have alleviated some of a child's language and/or motor delays.

Local transportation was a problem. Many families did not own a car or perhaps they shared a car with other extended family members. Buses were infrequent and bus lines shut down early in the evening.

My solution to this was to invite CEO's, Presidents, and Directors of nonprofit agencies and local funders to a luncheon meeting in January of 2000 where I shared a plan that I had been working on for over a year. Twenty-seven leaders from the community came for lunch to hear what I had to say. I proposed we work together to build a Children's Campus where children and families could access the services they needed under one roof. There would be quality early childhood education, health care, and comprehensive family support services that families could access without long lines and being placed on a wait list. The majority of those present liked the idea. However, there were two men who opposed the idea. One said, we had entered an era of technology and co-locating services was the old way of doing business. Another said, he would only support such a community effort if he were to direct it. He said, he was the one that "had the skills and knowledge to make the vision a reality." He intimated, "who was I to think that I could direct and manage such an initiative".

I was growing personally, as well. Things were changing at home. Danny got married in August of 1998. They lived nearby and it was fun helping plan the wedding, being with them, and anticipating our first grandchild, Jack Staker, born in May of 2000. This was a very fun time.

My mother's health continued to decline and my brother, Bill, moved in with her and cared for her. Bill is the oldest son in our family and there are unwritten expectations of the oldest son in an Irish family. Looking back, I think that was my mother's plan all along. Bill would take care of her and make sure that no one placed her in a nursing home. Mother led an independent life after my dad died in 1972. She made new friends and even tried going to work, but mother didn't take well to being told what to do and how to do it. She had her way. After all she would say, "What's Right is Right. That's Right." As she aged, she spent most mornings either at Redemptorist Church or the Don Bosco Senior Center. She enjoyed having coffee and sweet rolls with other seniors as they talked, only talked, about exercise and losing weight. She once told me there was this man who waited for her each morning at Don Bosco and brought her coffee. She liked his attention.

Even as she aged with crippling arthritis, at first using a cane and then moving to a walker, she drove herself everywhere, and the Lord help the pedestrian or car that got in her way. Her vision was poor and her foot heavy. Once lost on Interstate 35, she kept circling downtown Kansas City until she found her way to Don Bosco Senior Center. Her car had become her kitchen table as she picked up a McDonald's biscuit in the morning and perhaps a hamburger later in the day.

One day, I was at the neighborhood service station filling my car with gas, when I noticed my mother's car in the repair shop. The driver's door was missing. The service station operator laughed as he recited the story. Mother always opened her car door to look down and follow the concrete curb to back out of her driveway. The arthritis in her neck prevented her from turning her head. One day she opened the door a little too far and a bush took the door off. Another experience that ignited lifestyle changes occurred on a cold dark night in December. Mother called me at work to tell me that her car had broken down at 38th and Main Street. This was not the neighborhood to be in at 5:00 pm or after dark but, she explained, "I wanted an Arby's French Dip sandwich". Prior to Rodd and I reaching her a nice man had moved mother's car to the curb and helped her stay inside a building where she was warm.

Mother was also taking opioids for her severe back pain (she had fallen and broken her back a few years earlier) related to arthritis. She had arthritis in her knees but the arthritis in her shoulders was the worst. Once when I went to visit her, I found her in a semi-conscious state and thought she was dying. The emergency room doctor gave her an injection of Narcan, and suddenly she woke up and started talking with enthusiasm.

The children were all in their first jobs. David was working for a law firm in Kansas City, Danny was working as an engineer for Johnson County, Kansas, and Bridget took a job with a large accounting firm.

After working in Kansas City for several years, Bridget, the youngest in the family, decided to move to Washington, DC. Although this was Bridget's choice, it was a difficult move for all of us. In Washington, DC., Bridget was totally on her own, making new friends and driving long distances to work. She was working in Georgetown when 911 happened. 911 was a turning point for her. She decided to move back to Kansas City.

David, our oldest son, met Christy and became engaged within the year and married in August of 2000. David was 30 when he married and had waited not knowing if he would find the right girl. Now he was happy, and it showed. It was a joyful occasion. It feels good when your children are happy.

Major influencers and the lessons I was learning at this stage of my life:

I was still driving the 1986 mustard-colored Oldsmobile with vinyl roof. Work is very important to me and so is my family. The three critical memories from this period of my life that I frequently recall are described below.

- The night before Danny's wedding in 1998, Rodd and I hosted the rehearsal dinner. It was an exceptional evening with my mother, siblings, and even cousins from out-of-town attending. There were toasts and good wishes shared after dinner. I remember Danny's toast to his bride-to-be. He was so sincere and genuine in his expression of love. He had tears in his eyes. He called her, the "love of my life." When his bride-to-be spoke, she talked about the wedding. She was so happy and excited to be getting married.

I'm not sure why I remember this. All I know is that it worried me, even though everyone expresses themselves differently.

- A mother enrolled in Project EAGLE refused to have her son evaluated by a team of developmental specialists even though she understood our concerns about her child's expressive language. Months went by and the child's speech did not improve. One night the mother came to a parent meeting and brought her son with her. There were other children the same age as her son at the meeting. The children played together as the parents talked. After the meeting the mother came to me and said, "I want my child to talk like that child."

People learn in different ways, and you need to use different methodologies to help people understand and address any fears or misunderstandings they have.

- Bridget was living on the Country Club Plaza in Kansas City, Missouri in the Locarno apartment building; Danny's girlfriend lived at the Locarno; and my brother, Michael, lived at the Locarno. In such a big city of almost 2 million people, three special people in my life were living in one small apartment building on the Country Club Plaza. They were not initially aware of each other. What is the chance of that happening?

I don't believe things happen by accident. I believe that all **things happen for a purpose** if we are willing to search for it. **Be aware of your environment.**

I was also learning at this time:

Gather information and involve others in the planning process but always trust yourself. **Realize there will be bullies.**

Life changes as we age, and older adults need more help meeting their basic needs.

Relationships may not always be how they appear.

The reader's most significant memories and influencers from fifty to fifty-five years of age:

Chapter 12

2000 to 2005

Martha: 55 to 60 Years of Age

It was the dawning of a new century, and everyone seemed concerned that computers might not "turn over". There was the threat that computers might crash disconnecting us from the way we live and work. The New Century came in with excitement and fireworks, and the computers didn't fail. Life went on as usual.

I was sitting in the local Volkswagen repair shop waiting room having my car serviced when words and pictures on the TV announced that terrorists had hi-jacked commercial planes and flown them into the Twin Towers in New York City and the Pentagon in Arlington, Virginia. An additional high-jacked flight was still in the air headed toward the U.S. Capital in Washington, DC. However, within minutes word came that that passengers on the plane were storming the cockpit to prevent terrorists from crashing into the Capital building. It was September 11, 2001. 2,977 innocent people were killed as they were completing their normal routines for the day. Mothers and fathers were dropping off children at childcare sites. Men and women were purchasing a cup of coffee before heading to their desks, and others were on the elevator waiting for the door to open on their designated floor.

At the time, the federally funded programs I directed were housed in a federal building in downtown Kansas City, Kansas. Within days metal detectors, scanners, concrete pylons were in place to prevent anything from happening to the hundreds of people working there. Visitors were not allowed to bring any liquids or sharp objects into the building. This was the first time the United States had been attacked on its soil. Even though I had casually walked into the building where I had worked the last 11 years, I was now passing through a metal detector, my purse was examined for anything suspicious, and I even had a pat down if I had on my good watch or jewelry.

Life as we knew it would never be the same.

My brother Michael died on Monday, April 30, 2002, unexpectedly. As I look back, Michael knew he was going to die. Michael and I had not been very close in the late 1970's and 80's. Alcoholism had stolen his young adult years. One day after waking up in the Intensive Care Unit at Trinity Lutheran Hospital he told me that he said to himself, "I don't want to be remembered this way". He stopped drinking and built his respected and rewarding legacy as a founder and builder of Welcome House, a home for alcoholic men. We began to see each other again and enjoyed each other's company throughout the 1990s. On the Thursday evening before he died, Michael called to talk. He ended the call by telling me he loved me. I told him I loved him, too, not realizing this would be the last time we spoke.

Michael's employees and friends at Welcome House, where he was the executive director, sensed something was going to happen. Before he left work that last day, Michael finished all the business that needed to be done, including payroll. This was not characteristic of him. He died alone during the night in his apartment at the Locarno, on the Country Club Plaza. The Police called me at work on Monday morning to ask me to come and identify his body. The year before he died, he asked for a copy of the following Epitaph. This may describe how he saw his life.

"Here rests his head upon the lap of Earth
A youth to Fortune and to Fame unknown:
Fair Science frown'd not on his humble birth.

> And Melancholy mark'd him for her own.
>
> Large was his bounty, and his soul sincere
> Heav'n did a recompense as largely send:
> He gave to Mis'ry all he had, a tear
> He gain'd from heav'n ('twas all he wish'd) a friend
>
> No farther seek his merits to disclose,
> Or draw his frailties from their dread abode,
> (There they alike in trembling hope repose)
> The bosom of his Father and His God.
>
> Thomas Grey's "Elegy Written in a Country Churchyard" The Epitaph from that poem.

My mother died August 2, 2002, just 3 months after Michael's death. Her death was expected. Her life was celebrated at Our Lady of Perpetual Help (AKA Redemptorist Catholic Church) with traditional church music and mass. Close family were there. Redemptorist is where mother's parents were married, where she attended high school, and nearby where Mary Morgan had been killed by a streetcar. She was buried next to my dad, her parents, and her brother, at St. Mary's Catholic Cemetery. (See Appendix E for additional information on my mother.)

My brother Bill was the person my mother turned to after my dad died. For 30 years Bill helped mother with her finances and real estate matters. Bill lived near 45th and Madison in my grandparents' home until he moved in with mother in the late 1990's. As the oldest son in our Irish family, Bill had always been there for our mother, often sacrificing his own life and dreams to care for her. Mother expected this from him.

In 2003, Bill's health declined, and he believed he was dying. He had not been very healthy for years. During the 90's he had a pacemaker placed in his chest, cataracts removed, and frequent surgeries related to a constriction within his urinary tract. He believed now was the time to give his nephews, David and Danny Staker, his prized possessions: his 2 gold watches.

David received Ed Foley's watch. Ed Foley was my dad's uncle and Grandma Mamie's brother. The truth about the watch is this: Ed Foley was a barkeeper on 6th street, Admiral Boulevard. He would often give his nieces and nephews silver dollars that he got at the bar. He was accustomed to accepting jewelry and other items as payment for a drink. One day a patron offered up his gold watch for some whiskey. Ed accepted the gold watch and decided to give it to my brother, Billy, for Christmas during a rough economic time when there was no money for Christmas gifts. Ed's gold watch had never been his watch. However, it became a keepsake and a good story over the years.

Daniel (Danny) was given Grandpa Callahan's Railroad watch that he received upon his retirement from GM&O Railroad. Grandpa originally gave the watch to Bill, who gave it to his brother Michael, who gave it back to Bill. Bill then passed it on to Danny. This is a true keepsake earned from guarding the rails and box cars for more than four decades.

Rodd decided to retire December 31st, 2002, from his consulting engineering position that he had for 34 years. Rodd was a licensed professional civil-structural engineer. He was 59 ½ years old and eligible for retirement benefits. He had worked over a desk from the time he left the Navy at age 26 and wanted to do something else. He wanted to spend time outdoors. He had grown up in Colorado and loved the outdoors. He enjoyed woodworking. He can fix almost anything and make it look or work like new. He enjoyed managing his investments (his MBA had been worth the effort). He wanted to spend more time with his grandchildren and share his life experiences in the hope it would help them.

In anticipation of this career change he had quietly incorporated a company in 1997 to help senior citizens stay in their home as they aged. He invested our savings and managed our money and had time with his grandchildren. He was part engineer, social worker, investor, grandpa, and "sage". A man for all seasons. His career change was a healthy and successful transition and turned out to be rewarding for both of us. He was happy and still making money for our retirement.

Becoming a grandmother was great fun. I loved holding the new grandbabies. Even more, I loved watching our children parent. It was a wonderful time in our lives. By 2005 we had 5 grandchildren: Jack, Gabby, Ellie, Matthew, and Joseph. Madeleine would come in 2006 and Christopher in 2012. Emily and Quinn would become our grandchildren when Danny married Karen and her children in 2010.

I have lots of memories. Jack taught me new words like "ginormous". Gabby showed me how to care. Rodd had fallen while hanging draperies in our library and hurt his ribs. For the next year, Gabby never saw her Papa without asking, "How's your ribs, Papa? Are you ok?" When Matt was born, we went to visit him and bring him a present. His 2-year-old sister, Gabby, stood at the front door saying, "Don't come over here bringing him more presents." Gabby, at one year of age, came to tell my mother goodbye as she was dying. Gabby said, "She is going to sleep." What a beautiful way to look at death. Little children are a blessing.

Rodd's office, man cave, is a mess. His rule of thumb is that the door to his office must stay closed and locked, and no one is allowed in there. One day, when Christopher was five years old, he asked to go into Rodd's, Papa's, office. I quickly said, oh, no, that's where Papa keeps his money. With all sincerity, Christopher looked up and said, "I wouldn't take any."

Having grandchildren isn't all rosy. Rodd and I worry about our grandchildren and pray for them every day. There have been falls from scooters and wagons requiring stitches; hospitalizations for blood poisoning and concussions; episodes of croup and asthma; and of course, there was covid. Growing up in a world dominated by social media is stressful and the competition to succeed athletically is excessive. It seems that any means justify one getting what one wants. Where do children learn these kinds of behaviors? And, what about academics? What about meritocracy?

In the year 2000 when I was 55 years old, I began work to build the Children's Campus of Kansas City where children and families would receive comprehensive early childhood education and family support services under one roof. It would take the next ten years of my professional life.

From 2000 through 2010, I spent most of my time working to make the Children's Campus of Kansas City (CCKC) a reality. With initial funding from the Ewing Marion Kauffman Foundation and matching dollars from Region VII's Office of Head Start, consultants were hired to work with community leaders to explore the feasibility and sustainability of co-locating agencies that would offer services for young children most at risk of academic failure and poverty, under one roof. I believed that co-locating agencies under one roof would:

- Create a model of services where children and families could more easily access comprehensive services including education, health care, and mental health services under one roof. Families would be more compliant with their health appointments and fewer children would fall between the cracks with the services being co-located and coordinated.
- Establish a model early childhood education program within Wyandotte County for children most at risk of academic failure. It would be called Educare of Kansas City and serve as a model for other childcare sites, demonstrating how to provide developmentally appropriate childcare and early education.
- Enrich the professional practice of students and professionals by encouraging hands on experience and opportunities to learn the most promising practices in partnership with a team of researchers.
- Increase business efficiencies through shared meeting spaces and shared costs. It would also decrease the time staff spend running to meetings across town.
- Decrease agencies' operating costs and direct more public-private dollars into services for children and families.
- Keep the lease payments (money) in Kansas City, Kansas, and Wyandotte County where it was intended - to support the urban core.

Consultants were hired to manage work groups:

- Group I would Identify a potential site on which to build a campus where agencies would co-locate.
- Group II would Identify and evaluate existing national models of co-location highlighting each model's organizational structure, the pros and cons of co-location, and the process the agencies followed in creating the multi-tenant non-profit center.
- Group III would complete an audit of community agencies interested in the development of the campus and determine at what level the agency would support the campus.

The consulting process was successful. Possible locations for the campus were identified. Existing multi-tenant agencies co-locating under one roof from across the country were visited and studied. Four agencies emerged with a commitment to move to the Campus: Project EAGLE of the University of Kansas Medical Center, Juniper Gardens Children's Center of the University of Kansas, The Family Conservancy, and the Children's Museum of Wyandotte County. Ten agencies pledged to bring value added services onto the campus. More than ten other agencies pledged to support and participate in the collaborative developmental process. So, for the next ten years approximately 40 community leaders representing diverse community agencies and funders met monthly -over lunch - to advance and advocate for the campus.

The community moved forward with the belief that local foundations would fund this effort. The economy was good, and the funders were receptive to the vision. However, in the summer of 2002, there was a decision made by the Kauffman Foundation – the major foundation interested in funding our efforts – to re-prioritize what and where they would invest in going forward. Rather than invest in "community building" they would look to fund and encourage entrepreneurship globally. Although the campus would continue to receive funding for a few years from the Kauffman Foundation to explore the feasibility and sustainability of the campus, it would not invest in the design and construction of the campus building itself. I immediately began to look for other major sources of funding.

I began by asking local foundations for support. Local funders did not want to invest in CCKC or me. There was bias against funding a project in Kansas City, Kansas, where the CCKC would be built. There had always been conflict between the two Kansas City's. And there was bias against me. According to more than one source, since I had never asked local Foundations for money in the past, they would not invest in a person who had no history or record of success in managing money and programs. They went so far as to say, "who are you, asking us, for a million dollars." No one acknowledged that I had managed and directed 2 major federal grants worth millions of dollars, rating a perfect score in the full implementation of the grants, all while staying within budget. I had never needed to ask for money and that was my liability. Later I would also learn that money goes to people with money who will return the favor when asked. It is a closed circle. I was not a member of the club.

As it turned out it was easier to get money outside of Kansas City. I reached out to the Ounce of Prevention Fund in Chicago, Illinois. I had helped the leadership team there years earlier and I was hopeful that they might be able to help me, now. While in Chicago I visited Harriet Meyer, the Director of the Ounce of Prevention Fund. She suggested I give Dan Pedersen in Omaha a call. She gave me his personal phone number.

I made a cold call to Dan Pedersen as soon as I returned home, and he invited me to visit him the next day in Omaha. I drove to Omaha that night in my Volkswagen Passat and stayed in a local hotel. I made a dry run to the address Dan had given me to make sure I knew where to go early the next morning. I wanted to be ready and on time. The address landed me at a beautiful older home. The rest is history. Dan Pedersen was President of the Susan A. Buffett Foundation. Dan liked my idea of the Children's Campus and he understood what I was trying to do from my original drawing.

The first drawing of the Children's Campus of Kansas City used to describe and reflect Martha's vision for the Campus. A central building offered pathways for a coordinated system of services.

The Susan A. Buffett Foundation, which would soon become the Buffett Early Childhood Fund (BECF) pledged a million dollars toward the construction of the CCKC. Our team moved forward with RDG Planning and Design, engaging the Kansas City, Kansas community in the design and planning process. Preliminary architectural drawings were completed, and Intensive efforts began to fundraise $16 million, the projected cost for the design and construction of the campus. I was naïve to think I could just go out and raise $16 million. $16 million is a lot of money but I never once doubted myself. However, if you ask me now if it was hard or not, I will tell you it was very hard and only persistence and a belief in what we were doing saw me through. Plus, I think people got tired of me asking for money and decided they could get rid of me by pledging to support the campus.

Bill Dunn, Sr. and Bill Dunn, Jr., Bob Graham, and Mary Davidson (Cohen) assumed leadership roles in helping raise nearly $11 million. Additionally, Bob Graham acquired property from Bank Midwest at 5th and Minnesota Avenue which would become the site for the campus. It was located on a bus line, in the urban core and accessible to those who would be eligible for services. Mary Davidson Cohen pledged a million dollars and became the local anchor funder of the Children's Campus of Kansas City. Bill Dunn, Sr. asked the Mabee Foundation to support the campus, and the Mabee Foundation pledged $1 million. JE Dunn Construction, the Hall Family Foundation, the Kemper Foundation, and others made significant pledges. In addition to the million dollars that the Buffett Early Childhood Fund had given, they helped Project EAGLE, one of the participating building tenants, to incorporate their blueprint for a model early education program called Educare.

Bill Dunn, Jr. hosted many lunches and meetings disseminating the message and engaging unions and business leaders in the process. Bob Graham was successful in getting $2.2 million in Federal New Market Tax Credits for the campus. In the fall of 2008, groundbreaking occurred during a bad storm with high winds. The tent barely protected the 150 people that had come to share the momentous moment. Young children, their families, the CCKC leadership team, Mayor Joe Reardon, and others turned the first shovels of dirt. By the end of 2009, the land had been cleared and construction was underway. RDG Planning and Design, in Omaha, Nebraska, had designed the building and J. E. Dunn constructed it. This was a very smooth process with full collaboration and a successful conclusion.

On June 10th, 2010, 10 years and 4 months from the initial proposed vision, CCKC opened its doors and began serving young children and their families. The Grand Opening attracted almost 800 people with many coming from across the United States. As the ceremony began the sun came out and a rainbow appeared in the sky. Two years later, in April of 2012, the CCKC passed its last hurdle. The CCKC received word from the Court of Tax Appeals (COTA) that it was exempt from Real Estate Taxes.

Although this timeline reflects critical developments it would be incomplete if I didn't document that this ten-year effort was difficult and often traumatic. There were highs and lows. There were supporters and critics. Rodd continued to remind me and the team that this was a marathon not a sprint and the outcome would be worth the work. Critical to the success of this initiative were the roles and efforts of Allison Lundquist and Heather Schrotberger who provided financial, administrative, and general support.

The man at the University of Kansas Medical Center that I reported to at the time tried to take this project away from me. He wanted to be identified as the leader of this success story, while I did all the work. He offered a plan whereby the program I directed would come under the Department of Preventive Medicine at the University of Kansas Medical Center, where he could "assure its success."

He believed he was the one who should "scaffold" the effort and I would only succeed with him in the leadership role. I began keeping emails, letters, and minutes from meetings. And I enlisted help. I went to the Executive Vice-Chancellor of the University of Kansas Medical Center and explained the situation. The man of who I speak decided it was time to relocate to another University.

When I tell people that these were some of my best years, they look at me like I am crazy. Rodd and I took a second honeymoon to Ireland and Great Britain. We were gone for 3 fabulous weeks. The trip was a gift from our children. I was 60 years old; Rodd was 62, we had been married 36 years, and the children were all employed.

Major influencers and lessons I was learning at this stage of my life:

What do I remember most from these five years of my life? The following!

- My mother loved Reuben sandwiches from the New York Deli located at 70th and Troost Avenue. Swiss cheese, sauerkraut, and slices of lean corn beef covered with a special sauce fell between slices of soft fresh rye bread. I took mother one of these sandwiches the Sunday before she died. She sat on the edge of the bed and ate about a quarter of it. I think it was the last time she ate anything. Hospice was making her comfortable. She slept most of the time. I told my mother I loved her. Things had never been the same between us in the last 25 years. My brother, Bill, her son, her nurse, her friend, was there with her to the end.

I was able to say **Good-bye and I Love You**.

- I went to see the Director of one of the very publicized local Foundations in Kansas City. I had gotten to know him over the years. When I asked him to help fund the construction of the Children's Campus of Kansas City, he was very direct with me. "I don't believe in your program model of services. If you want money from me, you need to change your program model of services for the early childhood education component of the Campus. Rework the ratio of teachers to students and come back and let me know you did it. I will be glad to reconsider your request." I explained that an independent team of researchers had proven our proposed model of services was a success, and yes, our model of services was more expensive than other models, but data showed it worked. I asked, "is it better to invest in something that works rather than something that has failed in the past." He laughed and interlaced his fingers showing me, telling me, "This is the deal." I teared up. He loved it. His smile grew across his face. I kept my parking stub from the adjacent parking lot that he had stamped as a reminder, I would never ask him for help again.

Never. His ego and need for power were bigger and more important than any effort to help vulnerable children in the community.

Some people express their interest in helping the disadvantaged but all they want is power over others. Bullies grow up to be bigger bullies. Bullying happens everywhere. Bullying is when one sees him or herself as more important than another and is willing to lie or hurt others to get their own way. Avoid bullies. **Do the Right Thing**.

- To understand how other multi-tenant buildings and organizations across the country had succeeded I interviewed many CEO's and Presidents of such organizations. One woman I interviewed in Florida who managed a multi-tenant building and organization said I could build the CCKC if I had the passion, but it would take 10 years. I got off the phone and thought – no way. I don't have 10 years to give to this project.

Change takes time. Persistence, Patience, Purpose and a Plan are needed for success.

Other lessons I learned from this period of my life:

Some fears are externally imposed on us and **are unjustified.**

There is good and bad in the world, and we must work hard and work together to make sure **good overcomes evil.**

Take Risks. The old basketball saying, "you will miss every shot you never take."

The reader's most significant memories and influencers from fifty-five to sixty years of age:

Chapter 13

2005-2010

Martha: 60 to 65 Years of Age

2005 STARTED WITH my 60th birthday party at Lidia's restaurant on a snowy night with 40 friends and family. Family members had decorated the second floor of Lidia's with pictures, crepe paper, and fresh flowers. It was a wonderful night that I will never forget.

Happy 60th Birthday!

In 2010 my dream for Wyandotte County/Kansas City, Kansas, was realized. For ten years I had worked, directed, and managed the design and construction of the 72,000 square foot building that would become known as the Children's Campus of Kansas City (CCKC). Ten years and four months from the date I verbalized the initial vision for the Children's Campus of Kansas City, the CCKC's doors opened, housing multiple not-for-profit organizations and serving over 1000 children and their parents each year. The CCKC is a Beacon of Light for the community, offering center-based early childhood education, health care, and comprehensive family support services to the whole family. It is unique! It houses multiple agencies and services under one roof and serves the multi-generational needs of families, not just children. The primary goal of CCKC is to ensure children from disadvantaged backgrounds enter school ready to compete with children from more advantaged backgrounds.

Within this collaborative model of care, researchers and program staff use standardized assessments to track and evaluate each child's individual growth and development. This allows teachers, working in partnership with parents, to individualize lesson plans and respond to each child's particular developmental needs. Staff record the impacts of an intensive, intentional, quality early childhood education on the child's growth and development. However, the CCKC goes a step further. CCKC has established itself as a Platform for Change, sharing and disseminating the most promising practices learned at the campus. The CCKC vision was that "all children receive the early education they need to develop their potential and become the leaders in this promising but early 21st century".

It was during this period that I experienced "bullying" again. It is amazing the hurt that one person can cause. I realize now more than ever that being a bully is a lifelong practice by some. It is the way they get what they want. They need to win at all costs. Bullies believe they deserve to get what they want because of who they are and the titles they carry. Power is everything to them. One is never too old to bully. It is important to remember that with time the truth comes out, but the damage is done. It is important to call out the bully at the time it happens. Don't wait. Bullies use fear to silence others.

Rodd and I love to attend the University of Kansas Football and Basketball games. In fact, we have had season football and basketball tickets for over 50 years. People laugh when we tell them that we have 50-yard line KU football tickets. Who cares? Well, hope springs eternal. However, once basketball season starts everyone is excited to add their name to the list of who would like our tickets if we cannot use them.

Imagine our excitement in 2008 when KU was invited to play in the Orange Bowl. We had to go to the game! Mark Mangino was the KU football coach at the time. He was a big man with a big dream. Signs and tee shirts reflected the message, "our coach can eat your coach". For the KU fans, his size didn't matter. He was a good coach and able to motivate and prepare his players as no other KU football coach has been able to do over the last 50 years. KU won the game beating Virginia Tech. It was great fun. History will also record that Florida, the day of the Orange Bowl, January 3, 2008, registered one of its coldest days for the month of January in its history. We took the blankets off our hotel beds and wrapped them around us at the Orange Bowl game.

Imagine our excitement in 2008 when the KU Basketball team made it to the NCAA Final Four. Of course, we had to go to the game! We reserved a flight and hotel through KU Athletics and flew with other alumni to sunny and warm San Antonio. The home of the Alamo! The semi-final game was between the University of Kansas and the University of North Carolina. If you know the history of these two power basketball schools, you can imagine how heated and exciting the game was. With North Carolina losing we were able to upgrade our tickets for the final game. On April 7, 2008, KU beat Memphis, in overtime, for the NCAA Championship. It was a beautiful victory. Every year when I fill out my NCAA basketball bracket, I select KU as the Champion. I am a forever dreamer.

In 2010, Danny remarried. This was a very happy occasion, but I was worried. Karen had two small children, the ages of Danny's two children. Looking back, I know this was a difficult transition for them, but they were committed to each other and to making it work. Now more than a dozen years later they are happy and healthy. Life is not easy, and Danny would be the first one to tell you that. "It is what it is," he would say. There have been ups and downs in his life. However, he never gave up. He just worked harder. Danny is a warrior and hero in my eyes. As a parent, you live your child's joys and sadness.

Major influencers and the lessons I was learning at this stage of my life:

As you age the issues and problems you must address are more difficult and more personal. Three Critical Memories From this Period of My Life are described below.

- Harriet Meyer, President of the Ounce of Prevention Fund in Chicago, Ill, came to Kansas City to meet with potential funders and encourage them to invest in the CCKC. Rather than listen to the funders and understand where they were coming from, she admonished them. That did not work. Funders stood up in the middle of the presentation and walked out of the room. Ms. Meyer had not prepared well. One cannot come into another's state/city and tell them that you are a success and what they need to do to be successful.

Know your audience. Don't put your beliefs on another unless asked. Be respectful of others and inquire as to how you can help rather than tell them what to do.

- Danny came and told us (Rodd and I) that he was going to file for divorce. He had never spoken a harsh word about his wife in nine years. However, we knew Danny was having a hard time and sad.

It is hard to see your child in pain and not be able to help them. But **you can always be there for your child.**

- I can't sing. I found myself getting hoarse after I talked for a period. My throat would ache. I made an appointment to see an ENT physician and found out that the radiation of my throat as a child had damaged my vocal cords and the condition was worsening as I got older. This is one of the saddest personal things that has happened to me in my life. I have always loved to sing. I still try to sing sometimes in the shower when no one can hear me, and the water distorts the sound.

As we get older, we have less options in life and we must **adapt.**

The reader's most significant memories and influencers from sixty to sixty-five years of age:

Chapter 14

2010 to 2015

Martha: 65 to 70 Years of Age

If one lives to this age, he or she may face the fact that it is probably time to let go of some things. Or to use an old cliche, simplify one's life. For me it was time to let go of my job, not necessarily, my career interests. If we are lucky, we leave our jobs with honor and respect from those we worked with and the satisfaction that we fulfilled our purpose for which we gave or served. Leaving comes easier for some than others. It was not easy for me. It was like spaghetti without sauce or waffles without syrup or bread without butter. I loved my work, but I was getting more tired from the long hours.

I knew once I no longer managed the purse strings for the Children's Campus of Kansas City and Project EAGLE, I would lose the authority and influence to make changes and respond to new or continuing needs in the community. My role in the community would fade. I knew I would miss the professional relationships, the dialogue and environment that kept me engaged in building new and more promising practices in the field of early childhood education, and I would miss the assistance I had to keep me current with advancing technology. Thank you, La Shawn Williams. I will miss the exhilaration I feel when I am able to try something or build something new. Someone once said, "tell her she cannot do something, and she will prove you wrong." My mind continues to generate new theses or ideas that I want to act on, but I am tired.

I will **not** miss personnel issues. I will not miss grant writing and the stress of bringing in funds to underwrite the salaries of 80 or more employees. I won't miss the politics and competition within the university. Project EAGLE and the CCKC operated offsite from the main KUMC Campus so there were less political adversaries. Fortunately, there were many colleagues that worked collegially. It takes a social and professional network for one to succeed.

After retirement I was asked to consult on a few projects. I said yes. With one of those projects, I was asked to discuss how the application of research findings would improve program performance and outcomes. I spent time preparing my presentation but when I arrived at the conference, I was handed a sheet with prepared remarks, facts, and content that should be integrated into my researched and rehearsed presentation. So, I tried to integrate the unfamiliar, unrehearsed, and unexperienced data into my original paper. It was a disaster. I should have just presented my own paper that was real, genuine, that came from lived experience. Why had I tried to please someone else?

The second episode involved a call asking me to visit an early childhood education program in another state that was having trouble getting their early childhood program up and off the ground. It was my understanding that I would visit the site intermittently to identify the issues, make recommendations, and write my observations that could then be used to make personnel changes. However, when I arrived at the site the director's expectation was that I would temporarily move to their city and run the project until the program was stabilized and meeting expectations. When the director realized I was not there to take over and run the project she was more than irritated. I told her I had no such intention of running the program. I would have stayed at the CCKC Project EAGLE if I still wanted to work full time. Then I was criticized for accepting what I thought was strictly a consulting job and not an administrative position. I wish I had confronted the situation more directly. But I didn't.

When will I have learned all the lessons I need to know? When will I stop trying to please others but rather stick to what I know and be clear about it?

Christoher James was born on September 19th, 2012, just three months after I retired. Chris provided a bridge to my new life. What a blessing for me and the whole family. I had worked long hours after the other grandchildren were born and now, I would have time to spend with Chris and the other grandchildren. For the next 5 years I would drive Christopher's older siblings to school and occasionally drive to dance lessons, music lessons, and soccer practices. One day Chris, who was 4 years old at the time, was preparing to go to Florida on vacation. I called him on the phone. I said, 'Chris, I will miss you." There was a pause and then Chris said very matter of fact, "I'll be back." Yes, of course he would be back, what was I thinking. I was always glad to help when it meant I could spend time with grandchildren. Spending time with them paid dividends. I now feel connected to my grandchildren.

In the spring of 2012 Rodd and I drove to New Orleans for the NCAA final four basketball Tournament. The KU basketball team had made it to the Final Four again just 4 years after winning the national NCAA championship in San Antonio, Texas. We stayed at the Le Pavillon New Orleans hotel which was near the French Quarter and close to the Mercedes-Benz Superdome, where the games were played. The highlights of the trip include gathering every night at 10:00 pm in the small, quaint, and historic lobby of the le Pavillon hotel for peanut butter and jelly sandwiches and hot chocolate. This was a tradition started years earlier when a guest, registering late at night, asked for something to eat. I remember Jimmy Buffett entertained us one afternoon in the city park. The weather was beautiful, and thousands sang along and moved to the music. We visited Café Du Monde for coffee and beignets and devoured Muffuletta sandwiches. We had such a great time. It was a fun trip even though Memphis beat KU in the final game of the NCAA Tournament.

Rodd and I began to travel after I retired. We visited friends on the Jersey shore, Cape Cod and Martha's Vineyard. We took cruises from Alaska to Vancouver and another from Spain to Croatia, Montenegro, Italy, and France. We took a river boat trip from Budapest to Amsterdam. Rodd and I agree that our favorite vacation was our 3-week trip and immersion in Paris, France.

In the Spring of 2013 Rodd and I joined 13 other people on a trip to Paris, France sponsored by the University of Kansas. The trip was called **Immersion into Paris**. We became totally immersed in the culture. We stayed at the Aparthotel Adagio Paris Bercy in the 12th district. Although we had our own apartment, a small room would have done as we never cooked or watched TV. We were steps away from the Paris Metro, allowing us to visit museums, Notre Dame Cathedral, Le Marais, and Hemingway's Paris. We took the high-speed train to Dijon, the capital of Burgundy, and the train to Rouen and a bus to Versailles. We visited the Opera House, also known as the Opera Garnier, which was the inspiration for the Phantom of the Opera. We enjoyed people watching as we sat at tables on the sidewalk ordering more croissants and cappuccinos. This trip was special, too, because we made new friends. Two of the other 13 people on the trip were from Kansas City, Peter and Bev Newman. Together we walked the streets of Paris and rode the Paris Metro visiting Montmartre and the Basilica of Sacro-Coeur.

We decided it was time to upgrade the kitchen. We had the kitchen cabinets stripped and stained and replaced our dishwasher that had been out of commission for two years. We needed to upgrade the kitchen and held off buying any new appliances until we were ready for the complete renovation Looking back, it's good we did this then, as I had some health issues as I passed 70 years of age.

Although I cannot describe what I did most of the time, I was busy living. I was intent on ridding our household of unused furniture, old books, and clothes that filled our closets but never touched our bodies.

Major influencers and the lessons I was learning at this stage of my life.

The three critical memories I have from this period of my life reflect how emotional this time was for me.

- I missed my work and the benefits that come from being part of a team. I had worked for more than 40 years and I had used my skills to effect change that helped children and families. Now, I was questioning what was next.

I was learning that major **transitions in life are difficult, and it takes time to adapt.**

- I questioned why I felt it necessary to please others instead of being true to myself. I questioned why I didn't speak up and confront the issue.

I was **still learning** to be myself, to trust myself and realize people will either accept who you are and what you offer or not. It is important to speak up and tell others your truth.

- I often reflected on those employees I had to dismiss. Over the years I dismissed many staff and personnel. It had not been easy.

I learned to **be direct and address issues of performance often and early. It is ok and best to confront people with the facts and not let things go unsaid or unnoticed.**

During this period of my life I was also learning:

When you manage the purse strings people listen to you, and you have the power to make changes and influence people. **Money talks.**

It is important to replace activities in your life with something new when the old activities and schedules are no longer possible. **Find new ways to experience life and refresh the old and start new friendships.**

Everything worthwhile takes time. Some things cannot be hurried. Just like they say in the Bible, everything has a season. **Be patient.**

The readers' most significant memories and influencers from sixty-five to seventy years of age:

Chapter 15

The "Still" Years 2015 – 2020
Martha: 70 to 75 Years of Age

When I was younger, I swore that I would not become an old soul, ambling with a stooped frame. I would not spend more time in a chair than on my feet. I would have energy, stay out late and live the "good life." I had been told and I believed that these would be my golden years. Looking back, I wonder what was I thinking? Did I think I would die young, or did I foolishly think my joints would stay well lubricated, my skin would never thin, and my organs would overperform. I don't know which it was, but I know I prefer to keep busy and not think about certain issues. This approach has served me well. Some may say I live in a state of denial but keeping busy has served me well since childhood. And I "still" smile.

I wonder how I look to others. There are occasions when I accidentally see myself from a distance in a mirror and wonder "who the hell is that?" I hesitate when grocery clerks ask me if I need help with the groceries, and I am tempted at times to park in the spaces reserved for "senior citizens" even though I'm quite capable of walking.

I am leading the "good life," I just define it differently now than before. It feels good to be home, enjoying the art we collected, the pictures we took, reading, watching a movie, and savoring the meals I prepare. My favorite thing is having dinner with my husband, family or friends and enjoying a rich conversation over a glass of wine followed by a cup of decaffeinated coffee with cream. I find small periods of solitude helpful. However, I fear that one day I will have too much solitude or leave my husband to the quiet.

These days two flights of stairs have become my highway to work, where I am the happiest. My office is on the second floor of our home, where I write and read. The laundry is in the basement. Everyday I'm making the trip to and from work for coffee and lunch, and other activities that need my attention.

I call these my **Still** years:

I still imagine that I will exercise and regain my figure.

I still want to wear makeup and feel pretty.

I still want to get my ears pierced for a second time.

I still like decorating my home and I plan to reupholster the chairs upstairs.

I still like to shop with my daughter and girlfriends.

I still like to bake and cook, especially with my granddaughters.

I still want to take long walks and explore new trails.

I still love KU basketball games but don't mind watching the games on TV versus climbing the steps in Allen Field House or Booth Stadium.

I still like meeting new people and learning.

I still treasure the friends I have had since childhood.

I still miss work.

I still love reading the newspaper with Rodd on Sunday mornings while sipping and refilling our coffee cups.

I still love my children.

I still love politics. During this period of my life, I have had more time to explore and engage in politics. I voted for Donald Trump. I make no apologies. Mr. Trump is not a nice man. I cringed when he made fun of individuals with disabilities. I hated that he called people ugly names. I resented the fact that he generalized the behaviors of specific ethnic groups. It made me angry when I learned of his infidelities. But I chose policies, not Mr. Trump.

We must find new leaders in our country, people that love the United States and believe in real democracy and are willing to fight the extremes that are disrupting what makes America great. But I ask, why would anyone want to run for office in our country right now when they know that they, their family, and even their friends' reputations will be destroyed and their bank accounts threatened as they fight false lawsuits? Our country is suffering under the weight of regulations and too many rules. Something must change.

Trump's policies that I support:

- **I believe in School Choice.** Children should not have to attend poorly performing schools. All children deserve skilled teachers that engage the parents in their child's education. All children deserve teachers who will motivate them, encourage them, and believe in them while expecting the discipline necessary to learn. Children deserve teachers that teach reading, math, language skills, and science. Mr. Trump supported school choice.
- **I believe veterans deserve the best health care this country has to offer.** If a veteran cannot receive care at their local or closest VA Hospital, or if the VA hospital is not providing the highest level of care within a reasonable time frame, the veteran should be able to take a health care voucher anywhere he or she wants to get

the health and mental health care they deserve. Mr. Trump gave veterans' Health Care Vouchers to do just this.
- **I believe in Head Start and giving every child a good start** so that when they enter school all children are on a level playing ground. Mr. Trump expanded Head Start.
- **I believe in family leave** and Mr. Trump made this possible. Mothers and fathers can now take time off to stay home with a new baby, an elderly parent, personal injury, or health concern without losing their job.
- **I believe in U. S. Borders.** Those wishing to come to the United States should apply to come into this great country and then work toward citizenship. How come some immigrants must play by the rules and others can just walk or swim into our country? Don't we have a moral obligation to block illegal drugs coming into this country and sex traffickers from robbing young women and children of their innocence.
- **I believe in free speech and democracy.** This is more than words; this means being able to speak out about what you believe without censure. I do not believe in the "woke" behaviors or cancelling people just because they don't agree with what the Liberal press prints as truth. Once I listen to a speech, I don't need to be told what I heard. I don't need a translator. Once I have seen a debate or political speech, I don't need to be told what I saw and heard.
- **I support Historical Black colleges.** Mr. Trump invested in them for the long hall, something no other president did.
- **I believe women and minorities deserve equal pay for the same work as performed by men.** During Mr. Trump's presidency, women and minorities experienced the highest percentage of employment with minimum wages increasing across the country.
- **I believe in allowing terminally ill patients "the Right to Try"** experimental treatments that have not yet been approved by the U.S. Food and Drug Administration. Mr. Trump put this Act in place.

I still love food.

I could live on warm bread and butter, ice cream, pasta, and pastries! But at this age I need to be more careful. Doctors warn that too many sweets, and too many pounds, may cause Diabetes Type II. Not drinking enough water may cause me to become dehydrated, dizzy, and fall. My digestive tract has slowed. So, sweets taste good and are easier to digest than foods higher in protein. Then there is the awful truth that as we get older, we release more gas. Oh, so true. A friend, during a bridge game recently said, "I learned that I could walk and fart at the same time."

I still love spending time with my grandchildren. I remember the time Chris asked why he wasn't in all the family pictures hanging throughout his home and his mom said, "it is because you were still in the clouds". Chris' response was swift, "Why didn't you download me?"

Turning 70 has also brought with it new aches and pains and the realization that my chassis needed some new parts. I got a new hip and a new shoulder. Arthritis visits me on cold and rainy days and after I've worked in the garden or carried in bags of groceries. A heating pad and Tylenol work wonders. Life offers perspective. I know time makes things better.

Recently a dear friend, Mary Davidson, died. I miss her. She was a major influencer in my life. As the President of the Bart P. and Mary D. Cohen Trust, she also influenced what was being funded in the community. She loved to help others who were authentic and dedicated to helping the less fortunate. You couldn't fool Mary with talk and good intentions. She wanted to see how the money she gave to community projects was spent and whether the funding she granted made a difference. She had a fun-loving personality, but didn't hesitate to use four letter words when nothing else seemed satisfactory. In just a few words, one knew where they stood with her. She was unafraid to confront those in the community who were motivated by self-interest. Mary had a beautiful smile, beautiful teeth, and a sharp tongue, which she used to criticize and compliment a person at the same time. Mary was kind, honest, hardworking, creative, but practical. She had grown up needing to work to support herself after her father died when she was only 11 years of age and after an unsuccessful first marriage. Mary expanded my interest in the Arts and cared about me.

In 2017 the Staker family decided to visit our ancestors in Ireland. To prepare for this family excursion, Rodd and I flew to Ireland in the late summer of 2017 to secure lodging for 16 people, find a chauffeur who could transport 16 of us around the island, and initiate a relationship with our new founded relatives in Rostrevor, County Down, Northern Ireland, and in Inagh, County Cork, located in the southwest part of Ireland. It was a fun two-week vacation setting our plans in place. For the first time we met Paddy and Marie Murphy who are the founts of knowledge regarding the Coit Morgan Clan in Rostrevor, Northern Ireland. They have become an extended part of our family, caring for us as we learn more about our family roots. We met Susan Foudy and seven of her eight children in Inagh. Susan was my grandfather's step-niece. We saw where grandpa grew up and tasted the spring water that still provides fresh drinking water on the property.

Then in 2018, the whole Staker family - 16 of us - visited Ireland. Although the weather didn't cooperate every day, we had a wonderful time staying at the Slieve Donard Hotel in Newcastle, Northern Ireland and then at the Park House Hotel in Galway. The highlight of the trip was visiting family, enjoying Guinness now and then, and shopping and eating on the main streets of Galway.

When our family returned from Ireland in early July 2018 I went with Rodd and my younger sister, Elizabeth, to visit our older sister, Mary Helen, in Virginia. Her children had called and said she was dying. We spent three days with her. Her mind was sharp, but she seemed distant and disconnected from life and reality. The Irish have a saying that seemed appropriate. My sister had "turned toward the wall". Figuratively speaking, she no longer seemed interested in other matters. She continued to read her books and puff on Juul cigarettes in our presence. I believe she used these methods to hide her real feelings and prevent any type of serious "goodbyes". She died the following February, just 9 days before her 78th birthday.

Upon returning home I began to have constant neck pain. Two months later it was determined I had a fracture of my cervical spine, C-1. It took a year for it to heal. The cause was unknown.

The complications from having my throat radiated as a child worsened. My vocal cords were no longer straight but rather bent and I became hoarse when I talked for an extended period. I also couldn't sing anymore. My voice would break when I tired. This may sound like a little issue, but it made me and still does, very sad. I've loved singing my whole life. As a child I always sang with my mother and older sister as we washed and dried the dinner dishes. In high school I was part of the Glee club and sang with an A Capella trio. I sang at church, in schools, in the shower. I really miss not being able to sing. I tried taking speech/voice lessons, but the effort was great and the outcome disappointing.

As the new year 2020 began, my older brother decided to move to a Senior Community. He became part of the Independent Living section. Although this was not an ideal situation, he could no longer care for the home we grew up in. The home was in poor condition and a realty company bought the home sight unseen with the intention of remodeling it from the ground up.

It was at this time that the Covid Pandemic hit our country hard. For more than a year and a half most of my friends and I stayed cloistered in our homes. Luckily Rodd and I had each other and didn't do much during this time. Two years later I found that I had to push myself to rejoin the world. It became easier to just sit in a chair, read a book or watch TV. I think the whole country feels like I did. Now, no one wants to go back to work in an office. Everyone wants to stay home. The productivity of our country has decreased.

I still have the same girlfriends and am more grateful for them now than ever. They have shared my life and know my lived strengths and weaknesses. Friends are not as tolerant of each other as they once were. Tempers flare easier. Friends say what they please without the use of filters. In one way I like this, however, I would like to just bury some of the unpleasantness and stay nice.

I just read *The Midnight Library,* a novel by Matt Haig that explores a young woman's regrets in life. With each chapter the reader experiences what life would have been like had the protagonist made different choices/decisions. This is my time to review my life and wonder what if....

However, I am reassured that the person I have become, my potential, the gifts I have, my values, would still be there no matter which track, which life, I might have chosen. And of course, Rodd would still be there.

Major influencers and lessons I was learning at this stage of my life.

We never really know who is watching us or perhaps the impact we have on others. You will see what I mean as you read the three most critical memories from this period of my life.

- One never knows the impact you have on those around you. In just the last few years, two of my children's friends approached me and Rodd and asked if we had a moment. The first young man said, "Thank you for showing me that there are different ways to raise a family and for a family to get along. I learned a lot from you and your children." On another occasion a young woman approached me and said, "thank you for being a role model for me. I saw how you could work and have a family, too. You were the only person in my life that I saw do this." There are all kinds of family systems, I just didn't know how much others valued my-our family system.

Do your best. You never know who is watching and learning from your behaviors.

- "Am I dying?" That's the question my friend, Mary, continued to ask me. She would tell me she didn't want to die. She had so much more she wanted to do. I would tell her "I don't know". When she was hospitalized and dying, I told her that her father, who she loved and missed her whole life, was waiting to see her. I still couldn't bring myself to say, "yes you are dying". It was too painful for me to say. I did not want to lose this dear friend. Several months prior to this I asked her if there was something she wanted to do. She said, "I'd like to go to the antique mall". We made plans to go but when the day came, Mary didn't have the strength and was unable to go. Mary loved art, but even more, she loved to find a deal, a future gift for a close friend. She also loved Winstead hamburgers and cherry Limeades.

Savor your time with friends, offer hope, but tell the truth.

- I didn't quite understand what was going on with my sister, Mary Helen. She continued to act like there was nothing wrong and yet she couldn't get out of bed by herself, she needed frequent relief from the pain, and she wasn't eating. No one talked about her health in front of her. Once I told her over the phone, a thousand miles away, that she was dying. After that she wouldn't talk to me again. When I explained my sister's behavior to a family member in Ireland she explained, "She has turned toward the wall." It was her way of saying goodbye without saying it. Later, my nephew said, "Thank you for speaking the truth to her, someone around here needs to be honest with her". Who are we protecting when we don't speak the truth?

Make the best decisions you can at the time. Do not look back and second guess yourself. There is no way to recreate the circumstances and fully understand how and why you made the decision you did. Keep moving forward.

Other things I learned during this stage of my life:

Age doesn't define or limit our dreams, expectations, and intentions.

Retirement gives us time to reflect and do what we want.

It is ok to **enjoy life** without working professionally.

I love politics, cooking, and family.

Grandchildren are loads of fun.

Honesty is always best.

Life is short no matter how long you live.

Live your best life no matter where you are or who's looking. We are always teaching and modeling for others.

The Reader's most significant memories and influencers from seventy to seventy-five years of age:

Chapter 16

The Unknown-Ten Years into the Future: 2020 to 2025

Martha: 75 to 85 Years of Age

Looking 5 to 10 years into the future I anticipate that my life will change:

- Rodd or I may die and the other will be alone.
- Friends will become ill and die.
- Grandchildren will scatter across the world and "family" may not look the same.
- Maintaining our home may be difficult and Rodd and I may need to move to assisted living.
- There may be a decline in our senses: smell, sight, hearing, and touch.
- I may lose my independence and driver's license.
- I may need someone to care for my personal needs.
- There will be the unexpected.

However,

- I will watch more movies. I have a long list of "want to see."
- I will read more books.
- I will talk with my family on facetime.

- I will use Uber and Shipt.
- I will continue to pursue my "Stills".
- I will write more,
- I will continue to help who and wherever I can.
- I will bake lots more cookies and try new recipes.
- I will let others know how much I love them.
- I will be an encourager.
- I will drink coffee, eat lots of chocolate and ice cream.
- I will "smile" as I reflect on my life and memories.

I don't want to make this out to be a sad time. I have had the gift of time that not everyone gets. Although the future is unknown, I am hopeful that my past life experiences, the values and beliefs I have, my family and friends will be there with me as I make my next transition.

My Values:

Faith: My Faith and the Power of Prayer have comforted and sustained me throughout my life.

Love: I have had years with the Love of my Life, my children and grandchildren.

Hope: I believe I will make it to heaven and see my family again.

Family: I am blessed to have family.

Friends: I am blessed to have friends that I can share my life with.

Education: I have knowledge and continue to learn. I love learning.

Health: I know what I need to do to stay healthy.

Take Aways

I am Delia. I can Breathe…. I've told my story.

I am not looking for approval or disapproval from readers regarding the purpose or content of this book. Writing was something I needed to do for myself with a secondary aim of inspiring others to reflect on their own life and realize it is often the small things we experience in life that have the greatest influence on us. This Book helps me understand how I became me and is one more thing that gives my life purpose and meaning. We are living at a difficult time in history, a time when people are afraid to share much about themselves let alone speak honestly about their values and beliefs. Younger adults form inner circles with whom they will only share their lives. Isolation from others is growing. The constant fear of being cancelled, revoked, vacated, or ghosted keeps many of us below ground when it comes to leading with our values.

So, what have I learned from writing this book? I have had a blessed life with more good than bad. I am a person that has made positive contributions to the world despite mistakes. Family is the most important thing to me. I love my husband, children, and grandchildren. I treasure my professional life which provided so many opportunities for personal growth and ways to use my strengths. I still have many things I want to do in my life, and I have faith in what is to come next. I know what mistakes I don't want to make again. I value discovering the unseen in the ordinary. I respect routines as they allow me the time and freedom to be more creative and try something new. I am proud of my ancestry and what my ancestors did and accomplished. They lived not only for themselves but for the generations to come. It is important to stay humble and realize what we do, positively or negatively, will impact our next generation.

My approach to life includes 5 steps:

- **Be alert** to what's going on around you.
- **Slow down** and take the time to **reflect** on your life experiences.
- **Ask questions** and expand your learning.
- **Be brave** and share insights, beliefs and values, with others, and
- **Love yourself** for being **authentic while respecting differences.**

Reflecting on your life experiences can become habit forming. Reflecting is not something you do once. There are more memories and greater insights and understanding that come with time. It's important to repeat and internalize this process to really discover what's important and what is most meaningful to you; what is it that you plan to carry forward and intentionally pass on to others.

There are many positive outcomes when one chooses to practice reflection and share their life experiences:

- It may give one a sense of personal worth. I shared this book with one young man who said, "I don't want to look back. It hurts!" But looking back and recalling a memory or experience may be the beginning of healing and there may be a way to attach meaning that supports the growth that came from the pain one experienced.
- It helps one evaluate his/her purpose and direction in life. If we don't take time to consider what we are doing in our life we can never say that we have reached our goal or how we got off track. Remember, research acknowledges the best indicator of future success is past behavior.

- It may offer strength through challenging times ahead. Knowing you survived or made it through other difficult times in your life may help you realize you can get through the current situation, as well.
- It can build family connections and strengthen families. Bruce Feiler's book, *The Secrets of Happy Families*, states "Knowledge of family history is a clinically useful index of psychological well-being and prognosis."
- It brings those life experiences and values that you want to communicate to your children, families, and others to the forefront.

For those still wondering what a value is, I have defined it below. Values are principles or standards of behavior that an individual believes are acceptable and important in life. Individuals, societies, and countries **choose** values.

There are four steps to internalizing a value:

- **You must freely choose the value.** I choose to be honest. Values cannot be imposed on another.
- **You must tell others that you choose the value**: I tell my friends and co-workers that I value honesty.
- **You must act on the value**: I am honest in private and in public. I don't steal an apple from the school cafeteria when no one is looking.
- **You must consistently act on the value**: I consistently act on my value of honesty whether openly or covertly.

You can only claim a value if you follow the above process. None of us are perfect yet complying with and aspiring to these 4 steps is essential if you are to claim the value.

Sharing your life experiences with children is important. Encourage your children to share their life experiences and then help them give meaning to those life experiences. Don't avoid hard subjects. Tell them what and why you have chosen certain values Use my stories and rubric to ask others what they have experienced and value during the same age spans.

As I was completing this book, I decided to look up Eric Erickson's Stages of Psychosocial Development. What I learned from reading about Erickson's Stages of Psychosocial Development is that reviewing one's life or taking inventory at this stage of my life is a common practice. The Final Developmental Stage of Erickson's model is Despair vs. Wisdom. Erickson believed that as a person gets older, they stop and think about their life. If a person has regrets and did not accomplish their life goals, they may experience bitterness and despair. However, a feeling of completion or satisfaction at this stage may lead to a sense of wisdom and internal peace.

I hadn't read this prior to writing, but I guess Eric Erikson knew that I was doing what I needed to do to complete my life's work. But more importantly, his research might suggest that reflecting on one's life early and regularly throughout the age span will prevent one from getting to the end of life and experiencing despair. I also believe if one takes time to reflect, it will lead to less burnout and stress. Reflection will help you make better decisions or change behaviors that you don't like or don't work for you anymore.

Well, after all of this I still have questions, different questions now. Like, "If you enjoy and personally grow from the work you do, is it praiseworthy? It was "hell" at times building Project EAGLE and the Children's Campus of Kansas City, but I undertook the challenge with passion and persistence. I believed in what I was doing. Being a parent was difficult at times but it is what I loved most. Even though I know those who give of themselves to help others gain more personally than those for whom their efforts were intended, I hope my authenticity in my various roles was noted.

I also question whether values are replaceable or interchangeable? Society seems to have substituted exercise, Botox, electronics, materialism and self-absorption for what used to be the values of faith, family, and hard work. We delight in finding a new restaurant in the urban core where we can devour ethnic foods and interact with a multicultural crowd then go home to a homogenous neighborhood. We proudly set out our recyclables each week signaling we are doing our part to save the environment. Are these new and different values capable of building a healthy family, caring for the dear neighbor, and supporting a democratic society?

I must leave these questions and others for another time.

The Staker Family, 2019

Lessons from Seven Decades of Living

Please digest and absorb the following. Yes, this is another analogy to food, but never forget healthy food nourishes your body and I'm hopeful the following suggestions nourish your soul and help make you the person you want to become.

- **Trust Yourself. Believe in Yourself.** Don't be afraid to speak up and share your ideas. If you don't lead with ideas someone else will. Listen to others and consider their input but trust yourself. Be authentic.

Every time things were going well for me at work, or I was feeling like I was doing a good job, something would happen to remind me that I didn't have all the answers and there was so much to learn. In other words, I was humbled. I was afraid to hang up my diplomas, certificates, or awards, for fear someone would question my leadership, and I would be asked to leave. Then I would ask myself, "who could do this job better than me? Who cares more than me?" The answer always came back, no one. I gradually switched my feelings from feeling like I did something wrong to anybody would be lucky to have me work for them. My certificates and degrees went up on the office walls. I trusted myself. I believed in me.

Buffett once said, "Don't Bet against America." I say, "Don't bet against me." This isn't egoism speaking. I just work hard at whatever I try to do. We cannot control others, but we do have control over the decisions we make. And if you make decisions based on your values and sound judgment you don't need to fear failure. You will never disappoint yourself.

- **"There is no such thing in life as security, only opportunity."** Since college I have carried this quote of General Douglass MacArthur's in my billfold. It more than any other quote influenced my life and decisions. I took this to mean take risks and do not be afraid to try something, do something, be something. Don't be afraid of failure. Good things come from failures. Some say it was easier for me to take a risk because I had a husband to financially and emotionally support me. Yes, that is true, but I like to think I would have taken risks even if I was single.
- **Pay attention to the small things in life.** Listen and be observant. It is not the big things in life as I explained in the introduction, (birthdays, holidays, proms, graduations) rather it is the little things that find their way into our brain that lie there, replaying, and informing us – and make us who we become. Chance encounters, a reply to an email, working overtime, meeting new people can all make a difference. Be open to what is around you. I don't believe things happen by chance.
- **Always Do Your Best.** We don't know what is coming next in our life but when we do our best, we are always prepared for the next step or the next opportunity. It doesn't matter if someone is watching or if someone cares. What is important is that you don't disappoint yourself and you have self-respect. Remember all your life experiences add up to make you who you become.
- **Don't look back and second guess yourself.** You can never recreate all the conditions and circumstances that existed and informed a decision you made. You did the best you could. It is ok to change directions. Move forward and try something else.
- **There is no one set of answers for living a good life.** We each must find our own way. We learn the most from the mistakes we

make. Others can advise, offer wisdom from their own experiences but you must decide the path to take. Yogi Berra once said, "when you come to a fork in the road, take it."
- **Never give up on something you believe in.** Don't listen to those who say cut your losses and get out while you can. If you believe in something, fight for it. I'd rather go down fighting than just walk away.
- **People do things for people, not systems.** Build positive relationships! Build your social capital! I was successful because of the people around me. Surround yourself with people that are honest with you and tell you what you are good at and not so good at. All relationships should be reciprocal. People helping each other.

Before I donate or give money to an organization, I want to know who is managing and directing the program. I want to know if my money will help people or build systems. I want to know if the leader is planning to leave or can I count on him or her to be there and make sure the money is used as it was intended. I invest equally because of the leadership team and the relationship I have with them as well as the cause.

- **Don't be afraid to stand alone.** During the past 40 years I have often found myself standing alone because I would question a point of view or propose an alternative solution to a problem or an issue. I would speak out based on my convictions, my values, and what I believed to be right and wrong. I often went home after such an experience and questioned myself - asking why didn't I just kept my mouth shut and say nothing. However, over time it was that disposition or willingness to speak what others thought but wouldn't say that brought me respect both nationally and locally in our community. Maturity means we develop a strong internal locus of control and don't let others influence our decisions and behaviors. There were many days I closed my office door and cried. It is lonely at the top.
- **"Beware of the man who don't bitch, he is the troublemaker."** My husband loves to repeat this quote from a salty Petty Officer

who shared it with him as an Ensign, when he first came aboard the USS Merrick. The quote says it all.

- **Join and participate in something bigger than yourself.** Join a church, a book club, an Alumna Association, or a political party. Volunteer at a local not-for-profit. Belong to something bigger than yourself if you want to grow and be better. As part of the Joseph P. Kennedy, Jr. Foundation and the Buffett Early Childhood Fund and Educare movement I was challenged to think bigger and perform at a higher level on both local and national levels. I had mentors showing me the way and opportunities to work elbow to elbow with those I admired from a distance. External factors influence one's knowledge and possibilities. I loved being part of something bigger than myself. One interesting thing to me is that I never saw myself as the leader rather a part of a team and I liked pushing myself forward. Remember you can't lead without a team to follow. Be part of a team. It's fun.

- **Keep talking and stay connected no matter what happens or is said.** There was a time when my mother and other family members wouldn't speak to me. It was a very sad time for me. When my daughter and I had some differences she said to me, "Not talking to each other is not an option." She is right. Keep talking.

- **Establish Traditions.** It is an important part of life. I need things to look forward to in life. Create your own traditions: an annual trip, an annual lunch with friends, stopping for donuts after mass on Sunday, going to basketball games together, having pizza on Friday evening, hiding Easter eggs throughout the house. Traditions don't have to cost a lot. Involve the whole family in what they would like to establish as traditions.

- **Support a child's Early Years!** Eric Erikson, the developmental psychiatrist, said the most important responsibilities parents have to their children are, "First, survival. Then communicating values." One's early childhood experiences have a tremendous impact on how a child sees the world and how the child develops into adulthood. Children need help to understand what they see, feel, and store in their brain. Reading to a child can make a huge difference. Engaging a child in a book you are reading to them will help her/him build their vocabulary and succeed in life. Encouraging a child to use their words! This is critical. "Studies reflect that children who have a slower, longer, and more nurturing childhood may be the best way to prepare for adulthood. An article in the Wall Street Journal, *What Children Lose When Their Brains Develop Too Fast,* by Alison Gopnik, says that "Poverty, Stress, and ACEs seem to make children's brains grow up too quickly." (ACE stands for Adverse Childhood Experiences.)

- **Have Faith and Pray**. Make prayer a part of your day. Pray especially during good times. It's harder to pray when you're sick and not feeling well.
- **No need to be Perfect or Perfectionistic.** I'm not sure which would be worse, being a perfectionist or having to work or live with a perfectionist. As human beings we are attracted to others with whom we share similar lifestyles. That usually means someone that is imperfect. We look for "normal", everyday friends and colleagues with whom we have commonality and can relate.

My friend, Betsy, thinks well of herself and what she has accomplished in life. She brags about her children and grandchildren so much that sometimes you just want to tell her to stop. She over decorates her home every season, including pumpkins and pumpkins everywhere throughout her home during the months of October and November. She has an outside flag to announce each season and holiday. She loves card games and is the one who takes the time to read all the directions buried within the game box. She is a good teacher and can clearly express the game rules prior to starting the game. She never forgets her friends, planning seasonal get togethers. She shares recipes and homemade goodies. Betsy receives new videos to screen and often shares them with her friends. It is Betsy and people like her that make the world work. She cares about people. She cares about family. She communicates what she knows and what she has learned to help others around her. She goes to church every week. She and her husband raised three children. Betsy is the type of person we can all identify with. She is not perfect, but she defines what makes our country great. People who care about family, faith, and country. We all love Betsy's in our life. Betsy has been in my life since kindergarten.

- **Words mean different things to different people**. Words don't mean, people mean. Make sure to find out the meaning others are putting to their words.
- **Competition is a good thing.** Competition can bring down prices, encourage others to improve, and stimulate new and creative ways to improve existing systems. My friends call me competitive. They say that I like to win when we play cards. Well, yes. Why wouldn't I want to win. But I can accept losing and I determine how I want to manage a loss.
- **Be patient, things take time** All things pass with time. Things also look different as you age. My dream of building the Children's Campus of Kansas City took 10 years.
- **It is important to be intentional.** Be sure the person you are teaching or trying to influence understands what you said by having them tell you what they understood. Osmosis isn't guaranteed.
- **Change is good. T**hings may seem worse than they are. Sometimes it's best to wait out a situation to see what happens. But don't be afraid of change or the unknown.
- **All things are Negotiable**. You must negotiate up front. Prior to accepting a position be sure you understand the salary, the hours you need to work, and the benefits. Get the specifics that you negotiated in writing. I wanted to be able to leave my job at 4 pm each day to be with my children after school. I got it in writing.
- **Cherish your family.** I grew up in a home with 3 bedrooms and one bathroom (one toilet and one bathtub). Seven of us – mom, dad, Mary Helen, Bill, Me, Michael, and Elizabeth- shared the limited space. I cannot recall that we had a schedule, we just made it work. I slept in a double bed (the left side of the bed abutting the wall) next to my older sister till I was 13 years of age. As siblings we ate together, we attended the same schools, and every night washed and dried the kitchen dishes after dinner. But, even within these close nurturing quarters I am different from my siblings. Not

worse or better. Certainly not perfect. Just me. As I have gotten older, I understand the family system I grew up in so much better. I concentrate more and more on the positive and am grateful for my family.
- **Do the things you hate to do or don't want to do first.** Then you can enjoy the rest of the day.
- Your friends and work may define who you are so make sure you **believe in what you are doing and choose your friends.** Live a life where your values guide and define you.
- **Be nice to one another.** Kindness equals less stress in your life. You will be healthier.
- Continue to educate yourself throughout your life. **Education** is the great equalizer, and it keeps you young.
- **Take Care of Yourself**. My son, Danny said, "It's not the number it is the mileage," when I told him I was feeling old. You can't enjoy life and help anyone else if you are not healthy. This means you need to put yourself first at times. You need to get rest, and you need to eat well. Most of us think that it is impossible if we are rearing children and working outside the home. I agree. It seems impossible but somehow each of us must understand that we are important. I did a poor job of taking care of myself. I thought I could do it all and be everything to everybody. But it does take a toll. I never intentionally neglected myself, I just didn't think about me. It is ok to take care of yourself. In fact, it sets a good example for your children and others when you let others see you taking care of yourself. There are times when you need to ask for help. Others may benefit from being your caregiver.

Historical Facts and Influencers

Appendix A

My Maternal Grandma Didi: Delia (Bridget) Morgan Callahan
(October 10th, 1884 -June 15, 1957)

Grandma never wanted to go back and visit Ireland. She often said that there was nothing there for her. In 2005, one hundred and two years from the date grandma left Ireland, I and my husband traveled to Rostrevor for the first time. Rostrevor was beautiful. So green. The hillsides were covered with flowers and sheep. The North Sea, blue and calm, splashed the old stone wall that protected the main road through the town of Rostrevor from flooding.

I returned to Rostrevor in 2017, 2018, 2022, and 2023, to learn more about my grandmother and to meet grandma's cousins and extended family. One of the first things I learned was that there are many Morgan clans living in Rostrevor and each clan, singularly branded, differentiated them and their ancestral history from the others. Based on a handwritten note sent to my mother from Patrick Morgan in the 1960's, I was branded part of the (Quoit) Coit Morgan Clan. Coit Morgan's were known for their skill in playing quoits or skittles. Originally this game was played outdoors where individuals used a standard sized tree limb to throw at standing pins. The game is compared to bowling. Initially everyone thought I was part of the

Flaxy Morgan clan because of my hair color, and light complexion. I was not part of the Tailor Clan either, known for their skill as tailors and seamstresses.

Grandma had five siblings:

- Grandma's oldest sister, **Lizzie**, died in a house fire in Liverpool, England, along with her husband, John Carvill, and five of their six children. Her only surviving son, Johnny Carvill, came to America and settled in Kansas City.
- **Peter** Morgan (he was called Uncle Pete), grandma's oldest brother, never married and spent most of his life as a chauffeur for wealthy families in Kansas City, Missouri. Room and board usually accompanied his employment, so he never owned his own home. As he aged, he rented a room in a home near Grandma Didi, off 43rd and Westport Road in Kansas City, Missouri. Since my mother shopped in Westport we'd often drive by the home where Uncle Pete was living and see him sitting on an old painted porch swing, smoking a cigar – perhaps one that had been discarded by another with some life left in the butt. A loner, he isolated himself and was later placed in Saint Joseph Missouri Mental Hospital, by rule of a judge, at the request of his sister, Rose, and niece Margaret. When grandma visited him, she found him chained to his bed. I am told that he had hardening of the arteries and had become forgetful. A copy of Pete's Last Will and Testament reflects an indifference for his sister, my grandmother, Didi.
- **Jimmy** Morgan, the fourth born sibling, became the groundskeeper for Saint Teresa's Academy at 55th Street in Kansas City, Missouri. Jimmy moved his young family into the Boiler/Mechanical building located on the northeast corner of the campus. It is recorded that Jimmy planted and decorated the first Christmas Tree on the Campus for the Sisters of St. Joseph of Carondelet. One day while performing his groundskeeping duties he cut his leg and developed blood poisoning. He died a few weeks later. His wife and six children had to move off campus to

make room for the new groundskeeper. His wife later remarried and became Mrs. Delia Morgan Ahern.
- **Mary** Morgan was killed by a streetcar near the intersection of Linwood and Broadway, in 1906, shortly after coming to the United States. According to the local newspaper, grandma Didi and her sister, Mary, were out shopping for valentines when a streetcar struck Mary and carried her 40 feet. The conductor of the streetcar was found guilty of causing her death, and my grandmother, received $300 from the Kansas City Transportation authority. She used this money to bury her sister, Mary, at St. Mary's Cemetery and send her youngest sister, Rose Morgan, to St. Teresa's Academy, a private girl's high school located today in the Country Club District of Kansas City, Missouri. The same high school that my sisters and I attended half a century later.
- When Jimmy wrote and said he was coming to America, Grandma Didi wrote him back and told him to bring **Rose** with him**.** Didi did not want her youngest sibling, Rose, left in Ireland by herself. Once Rose arrived, Grandma Didi made sure her youngest sister had a proper education even though she herself had a 3rd grade education. Rose married James Bauman and had one daughter, Margaret Bauman. Margaret married Mr. O'Brien and had one son, James. My mother and Margaret – first cousins and once close friends -never spoke to each other in later years even though Margaret had been my mother's Maid of Honor at her wedding. Oral history suggests the Bauman family was embarrassed by my grandmother's willingness to work at unskilled menial jobs to make money.

Grandma, coming from the north of Ireland and living through the Great Depression in America, never wanted to be poor again. There developed a class difference between Rose's family and grandma Didi's family. The Bauman's were well educated and held professional degrees and titles. Later in life, I found out that Margaret didn't tell her only child, James, her life story. James didn't even know that he had aunts and uncles living nearby, let alone cousins sharing space in the same classrooms at Rockhurst High School.

Below are pictures of Grandma Didi's father, James Morgan, and her sisters, Lizzie, Mary and Rose. The pictures of Delia, Mary and Rose were taken soon after they came to America. The older woman in the picture with Lizzie was the midwife.

The Morgan Sisters

Delia, born Bridget Morgan

Mary Morgan

Rose Morgan

Standing (left to right) in the Loose Park Rose Garden on Easter Day are Mary Elizabeth, Billy, Grandma Didi, Michael, and Martha.

Appendix B

My Maternal Grandfather "The Mick": Michael Daniel O'Callaghan (July 3, 1881-May 24,1971)

In 2005 my husband and I visited the town of Inagh. The town consisted of two pubs and the Catholic Church of the Immaculate Conception. The church was built on the top of a hill overlooking the main road. By chance, the local priest was just leaving the church when we called to him. He invited us into the sanctuary where he opened the bottom drawer of a buffet and pulled out a church registrar that reflected my grandfather's birth, July 3, 1881, his parents' wedding date, the death of his mother, and the births of his siblings. It was unbelievable. This is what we had hoped for, our family records. There in front of us lay the lineage, the births, deaths, and weddings of the Daniel O'Callaghan family. I was overcome with emotion.

In 2017 my husband and I were fortunate to meet grandpa's step-niece, our cousin, Susan Foudy. She is the daughter of my grandfather's stepbrother, Anthony (Tony) Callaghan and Margaret Queally. Susan was born on October 8th, 1930. She had eight children, five boys and three girls. I have had the privilege to meet Edel, Mary, Patricia, Pat, Tom, John, and

Michael. Part of Grandpa's home still stands. It is the back portion of a garage now owned by John Foudy. His home is on the side of a hill, overlooking a beautiful valley. A natural well still provides drinking water and the perfect mix for whiskey.

Two of Grandpa's sisters came to America and became Sisters of St. Joseph of Carondelet: Sister Clementine, CSJ, and Sister Hershman, CSJ. They lived in Florida. Another sister, Delia Callaghan never married and worked for a priest outside Boston, in Worcester, Massachusetts. His stepsister, Catherine Singleton, lived in the Bronx, New York. His stepbrother, Anthony Callaghan, left his family in Ireland and moved to the United States and lived in the Bronx, New York. He also kept in touch with another brother, Dennis Callaghan, who lived in Dublin. Two of Grandpa's aunts lived nearby in Kansas City. Aunt Nellie and Aunt Bridget.

Appendix C

My Maternal Uncle Daniel James Callahan: Danny (Born in 1910 and died on January 30th, 1929)

Grandma and grandpa's only son, Daniel James Morgan, died at the age of 18. According to my mother, her brother Danny was a handsome ambitious young man who had great plans and dreams for his future. He had graduated from Allen grade school and attended Westport High School He had his own paper route and had bought a model T Ford and arranged to have his own insurance agency. With Danny it was appropriate to say, "a rolling stone gathers no moss." He was a pure product of his uprearing.

On January 29th, 1929, Danny wasn't feeling well. He had a fever and cough, but he still went out to throw the newspapers on his route. The weather was cold and rainy. Grandma had my mother help him deliver newspapers that day. When he came home, he went to bed and died the next day. Doctor Skinner came to their home and said Danny had pneumonia complicated by a heart condition. The doctor thought Danny might have had rheumatic fever as a child. Danny lay in rest in the front room of his parents' home. The funeral procession began two days after his death at 8:30 am as Danny was processed from his home to the church. The mass began at 9:00 am at Our Lady of Good Counsel Catholic Church and Danny was buried at St. Mary's Cemetery.

Dark days followed. The Irish who had been through so much, lost so much, suffered quietly. Grandma Didi never recovered from her son's death. She blamed herself for pushing Danny to work. Again, her past and grandpa's past impacted their parenting and relationships with their children.

Appendix D

My Father: William (Bill) James Leahy, Jr. (October 8th, 1912 – June 21, 1972)

From his early teens Dad worked as a caddy at local golf courses where he took up smoking Camel cigarettes. He did not have a very healthy lifestyle, and I imagine with his mother working for the city full time, and his dad, a state representative in Jefferson City, he was left on his own a lot. Dad developed a gregarious and winning personality.

Dad worked, his whole life, for a grain company at the Kansas City Board of Trade. Dad brought home his paycheck like clockwork every other Friday night and gave the money to my mother who carefully budgeted the household.

My dad's sister, Aunt Tootsie died at the age of 45 from Non-Hodgins Lymphoma. I remember her dying. I was not allowed to see her, although I was downstairs at Grandma Mamie's home and Tootsie was upstairs surrounded by family.

Tootsie had married when she was young and had a daughter, Kathleen Elizabeth Johnson. The marriage didn't last long. Shortly after that, Tootsie moved back home with her mother, Mamie. Mamie, my paternal grandmother, then raised Kathleen as her own daughter to protect Tootsie from a society that frowned on a divorced woman with a child. It was the 1930's.

Tootsie eventually married a successful editor and writer for the Sosland Press, Evan Jones. At the time the Sosland Press was dedicated to the grain, flour mills, and baking industries. It was a valued publication reflecting agricultural products and commodities. Evan loved and cared for Tootsie until her death. Upon her death bed, Evan learned for the first time that his wife, Tootsie, had been married before and that Kathleen was really Tootsie's daughter. Kathleen, my dad's niece, went on to marry Walter Puhr and had three children. Kathleen's daughter was named Kem: Kathleen Elizabeth Mamie Puhr, after those who loved and raised her.

My dad's younger brother, Joe Leahy, was born in 1919, and attended Rockhurst High School. He served in World War II as a radio operator gunner from 1942 to 1945. After the war, he graduated from Rockhurst College with a B.S. degree in economics. He worked for Harris-Upham/Smith Barney for 48 years. He married Mabel Irene and had five children. We were not close to the Leahy family. Dad's brother was a Republican and my mother was born and raised a Democrat. Her parents had supported the unions and fought for higher wages. Politics were raging within families, even back then!

I heard mostly negative things about my father's family as I grew up. I know that alcoholism was prevalent. There is a strong history of coronary heart disease in my father's family. I'm not sure if this is genetic or stems from one's lifestyle. My dad had his first heart attack at 52 years of age and for the next 7 years he was in and out of the hospital with heart issues and a stroke. He died at home, alone one morning on June 15th, 1972. I was 27 when my father died and my mom was 57. After that we never really saw my father's family again.

Mamie's brothers were Ed, Tom, and Joe Foley. Mamie's sisters were Ellen Victoria Foley Keenan and Frances Foley. Great aunt Mary Cosgrove was born to Ellen Victoria Foley Keenan. Great aunt Mary was my favorite aunt always bringing our family gifts and candy. Eddie Cosgrove was Mary Cosgrove's son.

My dad, William James Leahy, Jr. at 5 years of age

Kathleen

Johnny Leahy, Billy Leahy, Mamie Leahy, Tootsie Leahy

Mamie and Tootsie

Evan Jones and Tootsie

Appendix E

My Mother: Mary Elizabeth Callahan Leahy (December 6th, 1914 – August 2, 2002)

As I reflect on my parents, I wish I knew more about them as individuals. I know where they stood on issues related to politics, religion, parenting and education, but neither one shared much about their life experiences prior to having children. The focus was usually on us children, our education, our friends, or what needed to be done around the house to keep it up.

My mother was a first-generation child born in the United States of America to Irish immigrant parents. Mother was born on December 6th, 1914, to Michael Daniel Callahan and Delia Morgan. Her brother, Daniel James (Danny), was four years older than her.

Mother became an only child at 14 years of age with the sudden death of her brother, Danny. From that day forward (over 40 years) my mother would be the caretaker for her parents. Mother dated several boys she liked but her mother, grandma Didi, told them to get out and stop coming around their home. These young men had not met grandma's criteria for her daughter's husband. My mother's future husband had to be Catholic and agree to keep her daughter in Kansas City. Grandma wanted her daughter emotionally and physically close to her. Looking back, it is easy to see that

Grandma Didi was afraid of losing her only surviving child. The need to have her daughter, her best friend, close complicated my mother's life, demanding her time and attention. Being an only child and having full care of her parents as they got older impacted my mother's and father's relationship and what she expected from her own children.

My mother married my dad on September 10, 1938, when she was 22 years old. They had 5 children over the next 14 years.

About the Author

The nursing profession was Martha's gateway to teaching, research, writing and speaking. For more than 40 years her professional experiences included directing federally funded research programs related to early childhood education, parenting, teenage pregnancy, and, working with the Joseph P. Kennedy, Jr. Foundation on issues related to the moral development of children. She is married and still lives in Kansas City with her husband, three children and nine grandchildren.